*Presented to*

_____

*By*

_____

*On the Occasion of*

_____

*Date*

Cover image © PhotoDisc

All Scripture quotations, unless otherwise indicated, are taken from the HOLY BIBLE, NEW INTERNATIONAL VERSION®. NIV®. Copyright © 1973, 1978, 1984 by International Bible Society. Used by permission of Zondervan Publishing House. All rights reserved.

Scripture quotations marked NKJV are taken from the New King James Version. Copyright © 1979, 1980, 1982 by Thomas Nelson, Inc. Used by permission. All rights reserved.

Scripture quotations marked NLT are taken from the *Holy Bible,* New Living Translation, copyright © 1996. Used by permission of Tyndale House Publishers, Inc., Wheaton, Illinois 60189, U.S.A. All rights reserved.

Scripture quotations marked NASB are from the New American Standard Bible, © 1960, 1962, 1963, 1968, 1971, 1972, 1973, 1975, 1977 by the Lockman Foundation. Used by permission.

Scripture quotations marked KJV are taken from the King James Version of the Bible.

Scripture quotations marked TLB are taken from *The Living Bible* copyright © 1971. Used by permission of Tyndale House Publishers, Inc., Wheaton, Illinois 60189. All rights reserved.

Published by Barbour Publishing, Inc., P.O. Box 719, Uhrichsville, Ohio 44683, www.barbourbooks.com

Our mission is to publish and distribute inspirational products offering exceptional value and biblical encouragement to the masses.

 Member of the
Evangelical Christian
Publishers Association

Printed in the United States of America.
5 4 3 2 1

# MEDITATIONS FOR THE
# SATISFIED SOUL

*In All Things
Give Thanks*

PAMELA McQUADE

BARBOUR
PUBLISHING

# INTRODUCTION

*What is a satisfied soul?* you may be asking yourself. *And do I really want one?* Those are good questions.

Everyone looks for satisfaction in many ways and in many areas of their lives. We all want to feel fulfilled. But the person who experiences satisfaction on the job, in a marriage, and in other areas can remain empty if the soul remains confused, doubtful, or ignored.

Christians have learned that soul satisfaction is an unsurpassed delight, and it comes only from one place: Jesus. When we rest in Him, our spirits experience that long-sought fullness. Though it may be a challenge to do so, giving our lives entirely to Him, to direct in whatever way He desires, offers previously unimagined benefits.

Being a satisfied soul doesn't mean being self-satisfied—just the opposite. As believers, we find satisfaction in God, not our own efforts to gain His favor. Left to ourselves, our mechanical attempts to obey (and eventually we're bound to fall into automatic methods if we go our own way) fall short of His kingdom. As hard as we try, we don't have it in us to be perfect enough to deserve heaven. Only Jesus and the work of His Spirit in our lives can make the change we're really looking for.

Because the Christian life focuses on Jesus, and believers live out His broad blessings, in these pages you'll find many faith experiences: praise, joy, thanksgiving, overcoming, and so on. The satisfied soul is not a bored soul, but one that experiences both good and bad and comes forth victorious in Jesus.

May this volume touch your life as you seek to be satisfied in Jesus. There's no one else who gives the full life you're looking for.

# SATISFACTION GUARANTEED

*Oh, satisfy us early with Your mercy,*
*That we may rejoice and be glad all our days!*
PSALM 90:14 NKJV

You've probably bought items that guaranteed you'd be satisfied. If you weren't, the manufacturer promised, you could get your money back. But how many people bought an item, weren't satisfied, and found the company didn't live up to that promise? Instead of money, all the customers got were irritating responses or rejection. A promise is only as good as the person or group who makes it. We've often found, to our discouragement, that people aren't what they seem and disappear as soon as they've cashed the check or processed the credit card information.

But God isn't like that. He's always what He says He is, and He's gone to great lengths to tell us about Himself. He sent prophets, who wrote pages and pages about Him and His character. He even sent His Son to clearly show us what He's like. Jesus died for us to give a clear picture of how much He wanted to share our love.

Earthly guarantees often don't give us satisfaction, but when we read His Word and get to know His Son, we quickly comprehend the difference between people's promises and God's. His mercy doesn't fail us or make us miserable. As we accept it and live according to His promises, our joy increases, whatever turns life takes. Even when the rest of the world disappoints us, we can cling to Jesus and be glad to the very end.

Have you experienced God's mercy and responded to His love? Then your satisfaction is guaranteed. He promises you'll never be left or forsaken (Hebrews 13:5). Joy in Him will be your portion for the rest of your life.

# WHY GIVE THANKS?

*Give thanks to the LORD, for he is good; his love endures forever.*
1 CHRONICLES 16:34

It's not hard to accept that even something God says once in Scripture is meaningful. But what does it mean when He tells us the same thing over and over? The words of this verse appear in 2 Chronicles 5:13; Ezra 3:11; Psalm 100:5; repeatedly in Psalm 136; and in Jeremiah 33:11, for just a few examples. On top of that, the New International Version repeats the end of this passage forty-four times. Often it's combined with the statement that God's good or that we need to give thanks.

Think God's trying to get something critical through to us?

Though God tells us repeatedly He is good, and His love never ends, it's strange, isn't it, that every time a war starts, we start questioning that first assertion. Is God really good if bad things happen? Has His love changed? We can even ask ourselves these questions as we face challenges in our own lives that hardly rival warfare for danger. If life isn't going our way, we easily ignore the culpability of humans and throw the blame right on God.

Maybe God repeated this Scripture so often because He knows how badly we need it. Satan has such an easy time tricking us into believing lies about Him that we need to keep reality directly in front of us. So over and over, God reminds us of His true nature.

This is a good verse to memorize, because when Satan starts attacking, we can ask ourselves, *Why should we give thanks to the Lord?* And we'll have the answer, *For He is good and His love endures forever.*

# THANKS IN ALL THINGS

*Pray continually; give thanks in all circumstances,*
*for this is God's will for you in Christ Jesus.*
1 THESSALONIANS 5:17–18

If you'd asked me before I started, I would have said that giving thanks while my dad was terminally ill would be impossible. As I'd expected, caregiving was a serious challenge—emotionally, physically, and spiritually. But I hadn't counted on one thing: This trial taught me to pray continually—for wisdom, strength, and a hundred other needs. Because of that prayer life, I received blessings from God that I'd never expected.

Without God's help I could never have completed this task He honored me with. Alone, the work He ordained would have turned into a thankless chore. But the eternally faithful One combined the task with so many unexpected joys that thankfulness never became a problem. I praised Him for the steadfast people who helped in my dad's care, and I thanked Him for incidents that nearly happened but didn't. Despite a host of troubles, I received all I needed during that stressful time.

But better than any gift of support and faith, I received the bounty of Jesus Himself. For in my struggles, I learned just how close the Lord stands by His loved ones in trouble. Taking on a painful work for Him allowed me to become intimately acquainted with His gentle kindness and provision. Doubts evaporated as He stood by me through every hazard.

Facing a tough time? See it as a chance to learn just how faithful your Lord is. Then thank Him that though you can't rejoice that you face the circumstances, you can be glad He's by your side every step of the way.

He will be there for you—if only you ask.

# WORRY SOLUTION

*Give all your worries and cares to God,*
*for he cares about what happens to you.*
1 PETER 5:7 NLT

Some people tell you it's fine to pray for a family member's illness, but don't ask God for a parking space.

I agree, if you're simply being selfish. But when I take my cat to the animal hospital, I'm the first to request a parking space. My vet isn't in the safest neighborhood, and parking's at a premium. Frequently, I've had to drag the combination of an at least fifteen-pound cat and a fifteen-pound crate quite a distance. My muscles aren't that powerful, and Tuck hates being crated, so he slides into one corner, making the box hard to hold by its wire handle—it's a slow walk. Yet if I carry his crate in both arms, I often trip over the snow-encrusted sidewalk or stumble over its unevenness. Under such circumstances, I *do* pray to park nearby.

But I also accept that God may have another plan. If I have to haul my cat far, perhaps another driver had an urgent need. I recognize that the world does not revolve around me. When I can't park where I'd prefer, I've no right to whine or complain.

Still God says to cast all my cares on Him and to always give thanks (1 Thessalonians 5:18). So if I pray and get close by, I thank Him for that spot across the street. But if I have to walk, I give thanks that I *can* walk and that Tuck isn't dangerously ill. Meanwhile, I simply trust God to keep me safe every step of the way.

Doesn't He do that all the time anyway?

# COUNT YOUR BLESSINGS

*Surely you have granted him eternal blessings*
*and made him glad with the joy of your presence.*
PSALM 21:6

Count your blessings" is a popular phrase I've never related well to. The moment I try to list all God has done for me, I realize how woefully short my efforts fall. I can thank Him for my salvation, for the blessings of home, relationships, work, and ministry. But I know His grace extends far beyond that. Even if I spent a week, I could hardly cover everything adequately. And when I came to the end, all I'd have would be a mechanical list—the exercise itself would take the delight out of my praise.

Yet even joy-filled David didn't attempt to cram all God's wonders in a single hymn. Though he rejoices throughout Psalm 21, he hardly describes *everything* God has done for him. The king's adulation rings through much of the psalter—as if he couldn't contain it in one place or time. But his masterful adoration is more than a list of thank-yous. David knew a secret of thanks it took me awhile to uncover: Real thanks are tied to the nature of God. Here David offers gratitude to his Lord for specific blessings in verses 1–6 and ends describing God's eternal gifts. All the psalmist's joy cannot be separated from his Master's presence. Without God, the king understands, even the richest gain would be empty. To know Him deeply is the greatest blessing of all, and intimate knowledge comes with a lifetime of loving Him.

So instead of detailing every benefit God provides, like David I'll thank Him for a few big ones today and spend time basking in His love. As I look closely into my Lord's face, I can't help but delight in His presence.

# A FAITHFUL BLESSING

*And he blessed Abram, saying,*
*"Blessed be Abram by God Most High,*
*Creator of heaven and earth."*
GENESIS 14:19

Read through the story of Abraham and his family, and you'll often come upon the words "bless," "blessed," or "blessing." In the first book of the Bible, God made it abundantly clear He wanted to do wonderful things for these people. He made them a special group.

Yet sometimes being blessed by God still has its difficult moments. Abraham and Sarah received a promise—a child would be theirs, despite the fact that both were elderly. God would continue His people in an amazing way. But time went on, and the promise wasn't fulfilled. Like most of us, this couple didn't appreciate the wait. So they decided to take a hand in the situation, and Sarah gave her maid, Hagar, to Abraham. However, the child the maid bore was not the babe of promise, but a terrible problem for the little family and the nation it became. It's to Ishmael, Hagar's son, that the Arab nations trace their heritage.

God's blessing doesn't mean we can't make mistakes and pay a price for them. Like Abraham, we can get ourselves in awful trouble. But also like the patriarch, we can be sure God will be faithful with His blessing. "Abraham was now old and well advanced in years, and the LORD had blessed him in every way," records the Scripture, toward the end Abraham's life (Genesis 24:1). Despite the mistakes, God still loved him and gave him great blessings—including the long-awaited son.

God has blessed us with a relationship with Him. He is faithful to us, too. Let us walk faithfully in His way through all our days.

# CORRECT BLESSING

*"Blessed is the man whom God corrects;*
*so do not despise the discipline of the Almighty."*
JOB 5:17

These words, spoken by Eliphaz, a so-called friend to Job in his troubles, assumed the hurting man had done wrong. Eliphaz is one of those friends you'd really rather not have, because he hurts instead of helping. Yet while the speaker hardly had all the facts and probably didn't mean to bless as much as to condemn, there's still a lot of truth in these words.

As sinful people, we certainly need God's correction in our lives, and God *does* discipline us when we do wrong. Unfortunately, Job's friend felt *he* could take God's place and tell off the sufferer. His words fell far short of their intent. What was meant as holy advice became a stab in the back instead.

God does correct believers, and sometimes He uses other people to do it. But how the message is received can have a lot to do with the attitude of the corrector. Harsh criticism rarely finds its mark in any but a hurtful way. Those on the receiving end of such comments easily become bitter, even if the corrector meant well. But people rarely hear well when they're hurt.

Had Eliphaz used a humbler approach, offering a suggestion and asking his friend, "Could it be that you missed following God's discipline?" he would have offered better correction. Had Job erred, he might have heard the words and changed his life. His friend's words might have been a blessing indeed. But no self-righteous corrector, who is at least as sinful as the wrongdoer, offers God's blessing. When correction comes not from the Spirit God, but from a spirit of even well-intentioned condemnation, it's no blessing at all.

# BEST LOVE

*Because your love is better than life, my lips will glorify you.*
PSALM 63:3

Nothing in this world is better than knowing God.

Perhaps, with all the delights of this world, that sounds a little strong. You may be in no rush to enter heaven and lose the things you've worked hard for and the earthly endowments God's given you. But if you can remember back to the days before you knew God, think of the difference He has made. Would you go back to life before Jesus? I know I wouldn't. The emptiness of life without Him is something I'd never want to reproduce. No wise Christian could trade anything for that kind of life.

Once Jesus enters a heart, losing life becomes but a painful moment that opens the door to eternity. When we know Him, we need no longer fear what happens after death. Eternal delights cannot compare to anything here on earth—even the best of the blessings God's already given us. Our hearts are no longer earthbound, and we long to be with Him. When He calls, we cannot imagine staying in this world without His blessing.

Though we may not rush to leave the fellowship of friends and family, the beauty of the world, and so much more that God has given, like the psalmist we appreciate that anything that lacks Jesus is less than the best. Life here, without God's love, would be meaningless.

David had his priorities straight when he wrote this. Even being king of Israel, with all its benefits, wasn't better than loving God. So during his life, he praised his Maker. And in eternity, he's praising still.

# CHANGE OF MIND

*"For my thoughts are not your thoughts,*
*neither are your ways my ways," declares the LORD.*
ISAIAH 55:8

I don't know why this verse always makes me think of an office gossipfest. Maybe it's because gossip is so clearly not something God engages in, or because gossip's so hard to stop in its tracks. Perhaps it's also because the mentality that promotes it is so difficult to change, and it does so much damage to both the gossiper and the one talked about.

But when I think of God's thoughts and mine, it's easy to imagine I'm naturally about as mentally delightful to God as a gossipfest. I continually fall short of what I should be. Not only can my speech be doubtful, but the actions that result from it can be far from godly. I'm sure many Christians have experienced the same weakness.

If God had left us in that situation, we'd be utterly miserable. Even our best efforts at change fail easily, no matter how much we want to be different. But God offers us His Spirit, not just as an encouragement, but as a heart changer. He enters into us and begins to redesign that gossiping speech. Suddenly the things that come out of our mouths are truthful, kind, and fair. No longer do they reflect the blackness that painted our hearts, but the rainbow colors of His blessings. Our ways, too, become His.

I'm glad God's thoughts and ways are different from mine. Without that difference, I'd be stuck in the muck of my own thinking, without escape. But today, I'm free to dwell in His thoughts and actions. There's no better way to live!

# THE PERFECT GIFT?

*Every good and perfect gift is from above,*
*coming down from the Father of the heavenly lights,*
*who does not change like shifting shadows.*
JAMES 1:17

Facing a challenge? It's easy to wonder, *Where is God? Why did He allow this?* If your world appears to be falling apart, it's tempting to decide that God is ignoring you and even to wonder if He's as benevolent as you thought.

James reminded the first-century church that though circumstances changed, God didn't. When these early believers faced trials—and even death—they could trust that God was still giving them good and perfect gifts.

It may not seem that way at the moment. You may have lost a job or been forced to move to a new location. Life seems out of control, and stress threatens to overcome you. You can't see a good thing about it. But wait awhile. In a year or two, when you look back on this, God's plan may seem clearer. Maybe the new job will prove better than the old, or the challenge will give you new skills to further your career. The new place, once you adapt to it, may also bring you stronger friends, a better church, and an improved life.

Don't judge God's gifts until you have unwrapped the whole package. Often His presents are larger than they seem and take longer to unpack than you thought. But in the end, you're likely to learn that whatever pain you put into the situation is much less than His blessing—and without that pain, you'd never have had all God wanted to give you.

See, the gift really was perfect after all, and God didn't stop being good. For awhile, you just couldn't see through the wrapping paper.

# HEADING FOR HIGH PLACES

*Yet I will exult in the LORD,*
*I will rejoice in the God of my salvation.*
*The Lord GOD is my strength,*
*And He has made my feet like hinds' feet,*
*And makes me walk on my high places.*
HABAKKUK 3:18–19 NASB

Though he waited for an invasion of his country, the prophet still rejoiced. Fears of the damage his enemies could do could not deter Habakkuk from trusting in the One who saves.

Like Habakkuk, we need not despair in danger. No matter what our situation, we're called on to exult in God. That doesn't mean we nearly lose our minds and declare wickedness good. But like the prophet, no matter how bad the situation around us, we can rejoice in the One who has saved us. We, too, can visit the high, protected places by trusting our Savior.

Maybe you've seen someone do this. His world is damaged, and you'd expect him to be reeling from his troubles, yet praise remains on his lips. She's had more to contend with than you feel you could handle, yet she doesn't give up. Does sheer stubbornness keep these people going? Probably not. Because doggedness can only last so long. Weariness follows, and people fall apart.

But when God holds a person up, the weariness need not destroy. A tired Christian rests in God then continues on with a firm step. Through prayer and Scripture, refreshment comes, along with a new sense of purpose. Hope does not fail when it's put in the Savior.

Need salvation from a trouble today? Don't forget to thank God for all He's done so far and praise Him for His incredible faithfulness. Then get ready to move up to those high places as you walk with Him.

# HEAD COUNT

*"Indeed, the very hairs of your head are all numbered."*
LUKE 12:7

*Does God really know—or care—what's going on in my life?* you may be tempted to wonder. When you face a challenge or go to the doctor's office only to find you need to go through an uncomfortable procedure, you may momentarily question His caring compassion.

But don't fall into that trap of doubt for more than a second. You can thoroughly trust that God knows and cares for anything you face—good or bad. Not even a hair can fall from your head, Jesus promised, without His knowing about it.

It's not as if God is simply in the hair-counting business. Whether you're losing many each day or have a full mane isn't the real issue. What does matter is that God is so powerful that He can detail anything about You in a flash. (If He needed to, He could tell you how many cells make up your body.)

Even today, with all our scientific knowledge, we understand the amazement Jesus was trying to elicit from His hearers when He spoke these words. God knows all there is to know about each of us. But more than the technology of that fact, He cares about all that happens to us. Even when we feel hurt and insignificant to our world, we remain important to Him.

Next time you're tempted to doubt God's loving care, put a hand up to your head. If you want, start counting each hair, and before long you'll be feeling the amazing love He has for all His children—one child at a time, no matter how many tresses are on each head.

# NO LAST STRAW

*But for that very reason I was shown mercy*
*so that in me, the worst of sinners,*
*Christ Jesus might display his unlimited patience as an example*
*for those who would believe on him and receive eternal life.*
1 TIMOTHY 1:16

Even when Paul had developed a successful ministry and was teaching young Timothy how to pass the gospel on to others, he remained keenly aware of his own failings. After all those years, he still referred to himself as "the worst of sinners." The superapostle didn't tell the youthful pastor of all the wonderful things he'd done but described the failure that dogged his steps, even in the midst of great faithfulness.

Paul's teaching to Timothy gives me hope. After many years of faith, I'm still keenly aware of my own unfaithfulness, too. It's not that I don't try or don't care, but so often I still fall short. Just when I think I'm making headway spiritually, I discover a basic weakness all over again. I become distinctly aware of my own inability to fulfill all of Scripture's commands.

Even so, God hasn't given up on me. Like the apostle, I'm glad Jesus still has use for me, even if it's only to show how wonderful He is and how limited my own abilities are. Though I might richly deserve it, He has no plan of tossing me out of His kingdom when I've broken "the last straw."

Nothing separates me from the God who saved me in Jesus. No matter what I do, He's still faithful. So I'm motivated to keep on walking down His path, allowing Him to show His grace through me.

Like Paul, I'm not expecting perfection anymore, just forgiveness—and the eternal life He promised.

# PEACE ACCORD

*Let the peace of Christ rule in your hearts,*
*to which indeed you were called in one body; and be thankful.*
COLOSSIANS 3:15 NASB

Any collection of people who have a gripe, unsolved problem, or major disagreement keep coming back to it in many ways—they cannot live quietly with an unsettled issue. But bringing peace isn't as easy as it might seem on paper. The emotions that accompany disagreement can keep peace at bay for a long time.

Even in the church, peace can be hard won. You know that if you belong to one involved in an emotional struggle. If you don't have more than doctrine in common, your congregation is in trouble.

Paul defines what we need in order to have peace: a heart change that gives us "compassion, kindness, humility, gentleness and patience" (Colossians 3:12 NASB). But even our best efforts to make peace fail when, as hard as we try to forgive, resentment resurfaces in our hearts. Suddenly we recognize that our deceitful hearts refuse to go in the direction our heads tell us to travel. No matter how hard we try, we can't make our own accord, because though logic tells us to do right, our emotions head off in the wrong direction.

The only way to find real peace is through the one Jesus offers. Only He can make His Word truly rule our hearts, not through empty doctrines we cannot perform, but through a whole-heart desire to serve Him only and love others through Him. The compassion, forgiveness, and love that escaped us dwell firmly in us when we submit to His will.

That peace not only affects us body and soul, it makes us thankful for God's work in our hearts and lives. Finally, we feel peace in every part.

# MISSION IMPOSSIBLE?

*Husbands, love your wives and do not be embittered against them.*
Colossians 3:19 NASB

The "battle of the sexes" often pits men and women against each other. Even in the church, spouses attempt to make each other fulfill their "roles" by using verses like this against each other. Somehow I don't think that's what Paul or God had in mind when these words first met in paper and pen and were written down for all humanity. I'm certain it wasn't what God created marriage to be.

Let's not forget, when we read this verse, that God's the One who enables the sexes to live in this kind of accord. He wouldn't command husbands to do the impossible, though He might give them a hard task. Anything He asks a Christian to do, He also provides power to accomplish. There's no *Mission Impossible* with God.

I have to admit, I don't understand how God does it. But I've learned in my own marriage that taking any problem to Him in prayer can be the start of big changes. When my husband and I face the seemingly impossible and together share it with God, the way suddenly becomes smoother. Bumps we expected in our road never appear, or we manage to circumnavigate the worst of them. Solutions we'd never expected suddenly become plain. Things are never worse than I expected, after we share our way with God.

I want to thank God for a godly husband who has made loving me a priority. Embittered disagreements aren't part of our lifestyle because he's committed to love his Savior.

But God didn't end it there. He made this marriage mission more than possible. When we live in Him, it becomes fun, too.

# A PERFECT GIFT

*The LORD is my strength and my shield;*
*my heart trusts in him, and I am helped.*
*My heart leaps for joy and I will give thanks to him in song.*
PSALM 28:7

Have you ever felt as if you should give thanks, but your heart just wasn't in it? Perhaps at Christmastime you received a gift that was somehow less than perfect. You knew the giver meant well. His heart was in the right place, and you appreciated that. But maybe perfume makes your head ache, or the sweater he chose just wasn't the right style. The gift was well meant, but not perfect.

Giving thanks on such an occasion becomes difficult. The giver may suspect you are less than thrilled with the gift. But you still try to express the appreciation you *do* feel.

God never gives us the wrong gift. He never wraps up another item of clothing to fill our already overstuffed drawers. Instead, He recognizes the intangibles we never have enough of and presents them at the moment of need. When we lack strength, His is there for us. Protection? It's there in a flash, as we face a sudden danger.

A much needed gift received at the perfect moment is always welcome, even if it comes at no special holiday. God knows that—and understands the importance of timing for everything He gives. Nor does He wrap His gifts in shiny paper or attach big bows to them to get attention. His presents are always timely, always perfect, and are certain to be received with thanks by a heart that's truly His.

Your heart jumps with joy at His presents, doesn't it? Then whether you sing His praises or just pray them quietly, make sure to thank Him for each gift.

# DON'T FORGET THE SOURCE

*When you have eaten and are satisfied,*
*praise the LORD your God for the good land he has given you.*
DEUTERONOMY 8:10

God cared for His people throughout their journey to the Promised Land. Whatever trials they faced, they'd come through with His help, though they sometimes failed to recognize that truth. Whether it was manna in the desert or clothes that lasted for forty years, He never let them lack for anything they truly needed. They might not have flourished, but as they trudged to their new home, they were always fed and clothed.

As the Israelites came to the Promised Land, God knew all the good things they'd find there would distract them from Him. When the food required their own efforts, instead of coming directly from His hand, they'd be inclined to believe it resulted only from the sweat they'd poured into planting and harvesting the crop. They'd forget who made the plants grow and provided rain. So God reminded them that thanks were in order when they ate. Everything really came from the same God who'd brought them out of the wilderness into this rich land.

It's the same with us. When we face lean times and have to pray for every meal, we appreciate God's faithfulness. When the paycheck is slim, we clearly see that God has provided for the rent, the heat, and our clothes. But when our paychecks grow, it's easy to forget God is still providing. Instead we start attributing our wealth to "a good job" or "smart investing" or whatever.

No matter where the money or food comes from, the same Lord provides. Let's not forget to praise Him for the good land or good job or even the good investments that made it possible.

# NOT A MATTER OF MONEY

*"With man this is impossible,*
*but with God all things are possible."*
MATTHEW 19:26

When the rich young man approached Jesus to discover how to get eternal life, he must have looked pretty good to the disciples. This wealthy man tried to keep the law—well, hard enough to convince himself that he had kept it at least as well as the next guy.

What a shock, to him and the disciples, when Jesus told him to sell all he had to gain heaven. If such a fine-looking fellow, who had cash to boot, couldn't get into heaven, how could those who followed Jesus even begin to hope for heaven? They couldn't offer God gold.

Jesus pointed out that it wasn't a matter of buying your way into heaven. For more than one person, money has deterred real faith. Faced with the choice between money and the Lord, cash has won out.

If that's true, like the disciples, we may feel nervous. We recognize our own failures, whether with money or some other worldly attraction. Would we really give it up for God? The disciples recognized their spiritual danger and asked, "If this is true, who can be saved?"

That's when Jesus gave them the good news: Your salvation doesn't lie in your hands, but God's. What you could never accomplish, He will do in you. Then He gave them a peek into eternity when He promised that those who followed Him would rule on twelve thrones. Though we won't sit on the apostles' place of honor, the news is just as good for us: God has done the impossible in our believing hearts, too. Jesus holds our souls in His hands, and He will never lose one who truly trusts in Him.

# BLACK-FACED SHEEP?

*All we like sheep have gone astray;*
*We have turned, every one, to his own way;*
*And the LORD has laid on Him the iniquity of us all.*
ISAIAH 53:6 NKJV

The moment-by-moment struggle to overcome sin, when we're new Christians, keeps us mindful of how much we owe Jesus. As black sheep whitened by God, we can't forget our previous state.

But as we walk with the Lord, spiritual disciplines start to feel second nature. No longer struggling on each step in our walks with God, we easily fall into the trap of feeling cleaner than we really are. Comparing ourselves to others who still struggle with a sin we seem to have "under control," we no longer envision ourselves as black sheep. Suddenly, we're black-faced sheep: Most of us is clean, even if we do still sin.

When we start feeling that way, we need to take another clear look at our pasts and the Lord who took our iniquity upon Himself. Nowhere in Scripture does God imply we overcome sin apart from Jesus. No list of rules or spiritual guidelines can separate us from our wicked natures. If we think our actions make us clean, we fall into another sin—pride. Alas, spiritual cleanness has slipped away again.

The only way the color of our fleece changes is in the cleansing blood of Jesus. It's not a bath we take on our own, but a shower He rains down on us in mercy. And the good news is that in return for our sins He gives us total cleanness—not just outwardly, but of heart and soul, too.

To keep our hearts from turning dark again, though, we must take that shower day by day. Without His mercy, more than our faces is black!

# BURDEN BEARER

*Blessed be the Lord, who daily bears our burden,*
*The God who is our salvation.*
PSALM 68:19 NASB

Is there a burden you can bear that God isn't interested in? A problem at work? A needy relationship? A temptation you struggle with?

Whatever you face day by day, if you haven't brought it before Jesus, you're carrying an unnecessary load. You see, God knows our frames and knows we're made of dust (Psalm 103:14). He doesn't expect more of us than we can manage. That's why, even in the middle of terrible troubles, He can tell us that His yoke is easy and His burden is light (Matthew 11:30). God has a solution for every burden bearer: He offers to shoulder our hardships—all of them—for us.

That doesn't mean He promises a piece-of-cake lifestyle. He won't so smooth our roads that we never bounce around, but He will see that while we're driving them, we don't break an axle. With His power, we can keep on traveling the path He's set before us, even if we take a few unexpected detours.

Of course, if we don't want to give Him our burden, He will let us struggle along on our own for awhile. He won't insist we do things His way but will let us learn how heavy the burdens really are and discover our own inability to lift them. When our backs are tired and we can't take another step, He'll remind us that He was always willing to carry them for us and again offer to do it.

Is He reminding you of that today?

# A CHALLENGING LOVE

*Love does no wrong to a neighbor;*
*therefore love is the fulfillment of the law.*
ROMANS 13:10 NASB

Loving your neighbor as yourself, Jesus said, was the second greatest commandment, following only the command to love God completely. Then He commented that all Scripture was based on these truths (Matthew 22:37–40).

Loving God isn't hard to understand, even when we struggle to perfect our love. Though we often don't comprehend Jesus, we can accept that He's bigger and greater than we and knows what's best for us.

But loving a neighbor, especially a difficult one, that can be a real challenge. Will the action we're contemplating do harm to her? Will telling a family member what we think or how he's hurt us just cause more trouble or bring the resolution we've been seeking? Even when we want to do right, we often struggle with the details.

Love comes in many packages. If we need to hold back a harsh word, that's love. But love can also mean speaking the truth kindly, and gently, at a moment when a friend or family member is willing to hear. How can we tell which is necessary?

Before we take an action we can begin by testing our own hearts. Is there bitterness or criticism there? Then we cannot fulfill God's law. Are we suiting this simply to our own sense of timing, when another's not ready to listen? Then God is not likely to be pleased with that action.

Love looks more to the needs of others than ourselves. It takes into account their hearts, minds, and souls. Fulfilling the law is never easy for humans. It takes a God-sized heart to do that well—that's why we can only do it through Jesus.

# SHARING THANKSGIVING

*Give thanks to the LORD, call on his name;*
*make known among the nations what he has done.*
1 CHRONICLES 16:8

Giving thanks is just something between God and us, right? Though we might think of it that way, it's not necessarily so. David understood that, when he framed these words of praise, after the ark of the covenant had been brought into Jerusalem. At times, the prophet-king realized, God gives His people blessings that should be publicly proclaimed.

We do that today, too. Churches share the ways God has been faithful to His promise, and that truth affects an entire community, bringing some to Jesus. Individual Christians also share public testimonies that bring suffering people to Him.

Maybe whatever you're thankful for in your personal life isn't earth-shattering. Perhaps all the nations don't need to know about it, because to many people it would simply be a small thing. But that doesn't mean God wouldn't want you to share. If, during a worship service, you thank Him for the way He's helped you overcome a financial challenge, someone who's still in the midst of paying off debts may feel encouraged. Let people know God is faithful in family relationships, and those with such troubles will recognize His care in their own lives.

That doesn't mean you have to share every detail with the entire congregation. Everyone won't appreciate the details of overcome sin, and many well-meaning Christians have shared private stories only to face unexpected criticism. So be careful how you share sensitive information. Avoid misunderstanding by saving the particulars for those who could benefit from knowing them.

But when you have a valuable praise to share, don't keep it to yourself.

# WHO REALLY RULES?

*O Lord, how long will you look on?*
*Rescue my life from their ravages, my precious life from these lions.*
*I will give you thanks in the great assembly;*
*among throngs of people I will praise you.*
PSALM 35:17–18

Will God rescue us from trouble? When we ask for His help, and He doesn't seem to answer, the pressure cooker we're in may steam up our faith, too. Like the psalmist, we may question if God will come to our aid before we're cooked. In such a situation, we're likely to promise God anything, if He'll just show up on time.

But God can't be manipulated. Tell Him you'll give Him half your income if He gets you out of this, and He's not foolish enough to believe it. He can't be forced into doing your will, simply because you're feeling uncomfortable. He may even have you in that pressure cooker for a reason.

David didn't promise God half his kingdom when he needed help. He offered something that was probably much more valuable—his praise. God values our attitude toward Him much more than earthly things.

David promised God praise because he knew God would come through for Him, not because he planned to manipulate his Lord. Past experience had shown David that God could be counted on if he brought his problems before the King of kings.

When you need help, bring every concern before your Lord. Like David, you may explain every hurt that has knifed into your heart. Then trust that God will come through for you, and tell Him how glad that will make you. But don't put the pressure on the King, because it's He who rules over you—not the other way around.

# PROBLEM SOLVER

*Give us help from trouble: for vain is the help of man.*
PSALM 60:11 KJV

When you're in trouble, whom do you run to? Do you go to a friend who has more wisdom or money? Do you share with a counselor or a political leader? These people might do their best to help you. They might be kind, compassionate, or down-to-earth and try their best to give you aid.

But there are some problems people just can't solve, no matter how much they like you, how much education they have, or what authority they exert. Some issues are just too big for humans. Not everything has a quick and easy solution.

Yet even the seemingly unsolvable problems are not hopeless. Because there is One larger than all mankind who has solutions people would never even think to try. When everything else has failed, He is still waiting to provide the help we need.

Do you face a huge problem? Have you talked to wise people, even wise Christians, about it and still found no solution? You haven't even begun to solve it because you haven't gone to the greatest Counselor of all. If you haven't consulted with Jesus, you haven't really looked for the right answer.

So often, we accept that God has answers to all our problems but put off going to Him. Perhaps we're afraid we won't like the solution. But holding off on asking Jesus for the answer simply extends the suffering, because no matter what else we try, only His way will solve every problem.

Open your heart to Jesus in prayer and help is on the way.

# PROTECTION EXPECTATIONS

*God is our refuge and strength, a very present help in trouble.*
PSALM 46:1 KJV

I refer to our male basset hound, Belvedere, as our policeman. When I take him for a walk, he warns me of "trouble"—a dog walking across the street, a neighbor getting in a car, or a package being delivered. But barking at these less-than-dangerous things is really all he's good for. As soon as a person or animal comes close, he wants to make friends. His bark is loud and scary, but there isn't a bit of bite in him. My neighbors, who know him, just laugh at his noise, because they know how much it means. And if any trouble threatened, I'm sure Bel would be the one hiding behind me, instead of being a "help in trouble."

Though we may not seriously look to dogs to fulfill our protection expectations, whether or not we realize it, we all have them. We expect the police to intervene if a robber threatens our home—and hope they will catch him before he enters our doors. We expect our bosses not to allow anything harmful in our workplaces and take them to task if they do. But no matter how many efforts anyone takes, human effort never fully defends us from harm. Storms come and damage our land. Terrorists attack. No defense is perfect.

Only one Protector keeps us really safe, whether it's from physical harm, emotional hurt, or a spiritual temptation. Only One aids us in our pain, in the middle of the day or the wee hours of the night. Jesus is no mere barking dog but true protection from trouble and a companion in every trial. When we can't rely on a hound or a human, He'll stand by us faithfully.

# THANKFUL PRAYER

*And we pray this in order that you may live a life worthy of the Lord and may please him in every way: bearing fruit in every good work, growing in the knowledge of God.*

COLOSSIANS 1:10

If your pastor commended your church the way Paul praised the Colossians (1:3–8), you'd feel pretty proud of yourselves. But even while you were appreciating the encouragement on how faithful you'd remained, you'd probably understand that it wasn't the end of your Christian walk. The apostle didn't stop there—and neither would your pastor. Instead of assuming that the people of this church would never fail in their belief, Paul kept on praying that they'd know God's will and understand it (Colossians 1:9).

Doing okay for the moment, as far as Paul was concerned, was not enough for Christians. He rejoiced in the church's growth, but he didn't encourage successful believers to rest on their laurels. In the spiritual life things always change. New challenges come up, and God ordains additional growth every day for His children. Just when any of us think we've got things under control, Satan launches another attack, or God ordains a challenging service. No one can stop doing God's will and remain a faithful Christian. So though Paul was thankful, he asked God to keep the Colossians' spiritual lives moving forward.

When you've done well in your walk, be thankful that God's Spirit kept you faithful. Appreciate anyone who's helped you along the way. But don't sit back and imagine that you're at the peak of your Christian faithfulness. For the growing Christian there are always new opportunities to know Jesus and bear fruit that pleases Him. Keep on growing in Him today.

# CEASELESS PRAYERS

*For God is my witness, whom I serve with my spirit in the gospel*
*of his Son, that without ceasing I make mention of you*
*always in my prayers.*
ROMANS 1:9 KJV

I don't know when Janet began praying for me, but it was probably long before I even thought of asking for it. I'm sure she looked ahead and knew my husband and I would need a lot of God's strength to care for my ailing father.

I do know that for years Janet brought us faithfully before God. Even before she promised to, I discerned someone was praying for us. On days when I faced discouragement and my own prayers seemed so weak, I'd be uplifted. Though I could not have told whom, I simply knew someone had mentioned us before the throne of grace.

Many people had promised to pray for us, as we'd shared our need, but only after Janet had gone to be with the Lord did her daughter tell us, "My mother prayed for you every day." Suddenly the assurance that someone had been interceding for us came clear, and I knew who lay behind the strength I'd received when I was tired and overwhelmed. Rare was the day when I hadn't felt the power of those prayers that kept me going through my trial.

I could never repay or return the gift Janet gave us when she remembered us before God. Though I prayed for her, when she too was ill, it could never redeem her love and sacrifice. But we have some friends who are caring for an ill parent, and I understand something of what they're going through. I'll just keep praying for them, the way Janet prayed for me.

# IN THE PIT

*In your love you kept me from the pit of destruction;*
*you have put all my sins behind your back.*
ISAIAH 38:17

Scripture tells us God saved us from a pit of destruction. When we were headed for trouble, He rescued us from sin. That's not hard to relate to. We know how easily sin still grabs hold of us and the destruction it causes in our lives.

But the idea that God would put our sins behind His back—that seems strangely human. What would iniquities be doing there? Obviously, God could put something behind His back and ignore it. That could be part of the meaning—it's as if the sin would never catch His attention. But God doesn't ignore wrongdoing; He covers it with the blood of Jesus. Perhaps it would be better to think of His putting the sins behind Him—a bit in the way we do when we turn from them, and they cease to impact us. But even better, we should understand that no one can get to those sins without coming through Him first. Though Satan may accuse us, those sins cannot impact our eternal life unless God says so—and He won't.

Are we living as if our sin is behind God's back? Or do we fear that we can never escape sin, as it continues to mar our lives?

When we react that way, have we really left the pit? Aren't we saying God's salvation was only partial? But when we take sin seriously, seek to avoid it, and trust God has really done as He said, we begin to understand what this image means. Sin has less and less impact on our lives, and we live in the promise that we'll spend eternity with Jesus, not in a pit.

# TAPROOT

*So then, just as you received Christ Jesus as Lord,*
*continue to live in him, rooted and built up in him.*
COLOSSIANS 2:6–7

Some years ago, I wanted to move a sizable rhododendron bush from a prime spot in our garden and replace it with a plant that required more sun. Since my brother was visiting at the time, I asked for his help.

He hemmed and hawed a little, then gave his opinion: The large bush would be too hard to move. I didn't press him, but I wasn't sold on his idea. So after he left, I decided that however long it took, I was going to get that bush out of that spot. I grabbed my tools and started digging. Quickly it became clear that the bush didn't have a very deep root system, though it spread out some distance. And wide roots are easier to deal with than deep ones. Before long, I had that bush out and sun-loving plants in its place—all because the root system didn't go far down.

Like my bush, Christians can have several kinds of root systems. Some of us are shallow and narrow. When a storm comes along, we're easily uprooted. Others, wide, but not too deep, like my rhododendron, can grow large in the faith, but it isn't hard to uproot them with the right tools. Then there are the believers who send down a deep taproot, like a maple tree. Even a small maple sapling is difficult to uproot. It grips the earth with an impressive power.

We can't expect brand-new Christians to have deep root systems, but they can be developing taproots. God meant every believer to grow stronger in Him. We can never be too rooted in Jesus.

# TOXIC FAITH?

*Continue to live in him. . .strengthened in the faith as you were taught,*
*and overflowing with thankfulness.*
COLOSSIANS 2:6–7

Many years ago, one of our neighbors had a car accident that careened her car across our driveway, through a bush, over our lawn, and into a second bush. Only when it hit our front steps did it halt.

Insurance took care of most of the problem, but years later, no matter what we put next to the steps, that plant would die. Something toxic must have leaked into the soil and poisoned anything we tried to place there.

When you've developed the faith taproot described in Colossians 2:6–7, you are meant to grow spiritually. But if you've put your roots down in the wrong soil—or soil that has a toxin in it—you'll wither and die, just like the plants in my plot. Spiritual toxins like heresy, legalistic beliefs, and wrong doctrines can destroy a Christian just as surely as bad soil or water kills a plant.

Paul didn't want the Colossians trusting in the wrong thing; that's why he told them to be strengthened in "the faith as you were taught." Not just the ideas of some passing preacher but the faith the apostles had received from Jesus would make them grow deep in the good things God had to offer.

Like those first-century believers, we need to look carefully at what every preacher says. Anything not agreeing with Scripture should be suspect—we don't want to tap into that idea and need to be careful about anyone who supports it. But when we're in God's Word, believing what it says and acting on those truths, not only will we be strong in Jesus, we'll overflow with thanks to the God who worked His power in our lives.

# SPIRITUAL COMPETITION?

*I always thank God for you because of his grace*
*given you in Christ Jesus.*
1 CORINTHIANS 1:4

When God gives another, younger Christian a great blessing, are you thankful or jealous? Paul felt thankful that a powerful blessing had fallen on the Corinthians. Though they were still young believers and didn't have it all together, the correction Paul administered in this letter was not done from a sense of jealousy. A few verses later, the apostle lets them know he isn't interested in making himself famous, but in lifting up Jesus. From one who had worked to develop thriving churches on two continents, his sense of humility is amazing.

God doesn't give any of us blessings to start a game of "Who Can Top This?" Competition for "spiritual position" just isn't part of His plan. Realizing the futility of such desires, Paul committed himself to doing the real job—reaching people for Jesus—instead of trying to make himself look good.

How many of our churches could learn from Paul's example? How often we could benefit from following in his footsteps, lifting up others who are new to the faith and need encouragement, as well as another lesson in what it means to love Jesus.

Is there a new Christian in your church who's doing great things for God, even though he doesn't know the Scriptures as well as you do? Come alongside him and encourage him. Offer to help him however you can. Make it a priority to pray for him. Then thank God for the blessings He's given you, too, and make the most of your gifts, so that together you can lead people to Jesus.

# NO LOST WORD

*Devote yourselves to prayer, being watchful and thankful.*
COLOSSIANS 4:2

These few words contain many ideas—something the Bible excels in. No word is lost, in Scripture, or unimportant. A brief phrase, like this one, can have an amazing depth of meaning.

Devoting ourselves to prayer—that command is perfectly clear. Without prayer, we cannot have a close relationship with God. The apostle knew the benefit of prayer on our spiritual lives, so of course he'd say that. But watchful and thankful—what do they mean? Aren't these unusual concepts to put together in such a sentence?

When Paul wrote the Colossians, some unidentified heresy was a great danger to the young church. These wrong teachings had enough impact to make the apostle write the congregation to refute them. Paul warned believers to beware of trusting in human traditions instead of God's truth (see Colossians 2:8) and repeated the tenets of the faith that would keep them firm in Christ. Then he described a faithful Christian lifestyle. In a few pages, the apostle gives a picture of what a Christian should and shouldn't be.

That's information that's as necessary to today's church as it was in the first century. We, too, face erroneous teachings and need Paul's warning to be watchful about what we trust in. If we don't know what we believe, anyone can mislead us. But with those Colossian truths, we can develop a faithful Christian lifestyle that blesses us through all our years. As we learn these truths and put them to work in our lives, we receive many blessings and appreciate them. So we go to prayer and thank our Lord for all He's done.

All three ideas in one place, just as in one verse. Imagine, Scripture said it all in just eight words!

# IMPORTANT MISSION

*Then [the older women] can train the younger women to love*
*their husbands and children, to be self-controlled and pure,*
*to be busy at home, to be kind, and to be subject to their husbands,*
*so that no one will malign the word of God.*
TITUS 2:4–5

What a counter-cultural statement this is for today's woman! Everyone is so busy, who has time for a female mentor? In many working households, it's hard enough to find time to spend some time with God, love your husband, and feed the kids, much less add a relationship with another woman to your schedule. Even with labor-saving devices, women have to spend a certain amount of time washing clothes, cleaning the house, and caring for children. Since most husbands don't relish the idea of adding housework to their crowded agendas, few women find help there. So those who work full time end up with hopelessly crowded lives.

Modern society may not place much importance on a woman's family role. It tells us the workplace is of primary importance; what you do at home doesn't much matter. But that's not the biblical view. God sees what a woman does at home as an important mission. Why? Because a badly lived home life may cause others to malign God's Word.

So if your home life is out of control, why not take the advice of Scripture and find a kindly older Christian woman who can help you put your home in perspective. You may not always agree on every detail, but share ideas on everything from quick recipes to deep relationships. Give a call, write a note, or meet with your mentor whenever you can—and complete that important mission God's placed in your hands.

# NEVER GIVE UP

*Grace and peace to you from God our Father
and the Lord Jesus Christ.*

1 CORINTHIANS 1:3

If anyone really needed grace and peace, it was the Corinthians. Paul's letters to them describe a church that constantly faced problems that might make a lot of modern-day believers move to another congregation. Sin didn't creep into that church, it marched right up to the altar.

Yet when the apostle wished grace and peace on these young Christians, he wasn't being facetious. The first eight verses of this chapter make that clear. Paul was more interested in putting them on the right path than handing them a harsh critique. Any critical comments are designed to show them a better way in Jesus.

We, too, may have days when we need huge quantities of God's grace and peace. A relationship gone awry, a bad choice that we have to live with, or a seemingly impossible work situation has derailed our lives. We know what's wrong, and we're not looking for anyone to simply delight in telling us how bad we are. Instead, we need a solution.

Like those Corinthians, when we get help, we'll have to face the bad news and admit what wrongs we've done. But we also need someone like Paul, who won't give up on us. We want one of God's people to come to us with grace and peace, help us find the right path, and aid us in walking down it for the rest of our lives.

No Christian is beyond God's grace and peace. Paul told that to the Corinthians, and he's telling it to us, too. Jesus picks up fallen people with His unending grace and mercy. He never, never, never gives up on a child who calls out to Him.

# PRAYER PARTNERS

*On him we have set our hope that he will continue to deliver us,*
*as you help us by your prayers.*
*Then many will give thanks on our behalf for the gracious favor*
*granted us in answer to the prayers of many.*
2 CORINTHIANS 1:10–11

Paul deeply trusted that God would help his ministry, but that didn't mean he didn't need the prayers of the Corinthians. Though these young Christians struggled in their own walk with Christ and the apostle had great spiritual depth, Paul did not discount the value of their petitions in God's plans.

How perfect the Corinthians' Christianity was didn't seem to concern Paul. He knew that both he and the members of that church were sinners. Before God, neither commanded perfection. Perhaps Paul understood that the spiritual victories these Christians had begun to experience could help him. The Corinthians might have insight into the hearts of those whom he hoped to reach.

If the apostle needed the prayers of others, how much we also do. Though we may trust in God to provide for us, deal with illness and doubt, and guide us in trouble, like the apostle, we are not designed to live the Christian life alone. God made us for communion with both Himself and other believers. We work best, as Christians, when we support one another in trials and troubles and rejoice at the good things in our lives.

When we need the petitions of others, we need not seek out the perfect prayer warrior, but ask those whom God has given to us in communion. As they bring our concerns before Him, He faithfully answers. Then many others, whom those prayers affect, will also give thanks.

# A GOOD FRIEND

*And let us consider one another in order*
*to stir up love and good works.*
HEBREWS 10:24 NKJV

Would other Christians be able to give you a reputation for stirring them up in the faith? By being around you, are they challenged to serve God in their daily lives, at work, in the home, and among friends?

If so, your friends have found a really good friend, one who cares for them deeply and wants to see the best in them. How many people—even Christians—have friends who love to tell them all the dirt, get into spats, and make life difficult? They're just the opposite kind of person who can help them grow in Christ. Maybe that's the kind of person they've been drawn to because they've never had a better example of what friendship should be.

A really good friend—the kind Jesus wants to create—can be hard to find. It takes commitment to a person's best interests to stir her up to love and good works, and it needs to be done gently, if it's going to work. People don't make friends with those who barge into their lives and tell them what to do. But a church friend who listens, kindly comments on a problem, and encourages could be of great value. If that friend stands by you in the good works that follow, she will receive a special place in your heart.

Whether it's a close friend or someone you know slightly from church, gently stir up love and good works. Then God, who is Best Friend to you both, will be pleased.

# THE GREATEST REWARD

*Therefore do not cast away your confidence,*
*which has great reward.*
HEBREWS 10:35 NKJV

In the working world, confidence gets a lot of appreciation. If you seem to think well of yourself, can stand up to opposition, and deal well with others, you're likely to get ahead. Those who are shy and uncertain of their own abilities have a harder time making it up the corporate ladder.

The rewards of social confidence can seem impressive. It may bring a larger car or house, increased social connections, and more work-related responsibilities. But none of those things is the "great reward" this Scripture speaks of. The writer of Hebrews is talking about the final spiritual reward, heaven. To his readers, who struggled in a world where their confidence in Jesus didn't get raves, the truth that faith brings a reward far beyond any social skill was more of a life-saver than a rescue helicopter to a person adrift in a choppy sea. As they felt themselves going down for the third time, God reminded them that even going down in this world didn't settle things in the next one.

Like those fearful first-century Christians, if we believe in Jesus, we've been cast a lifeline. We've connected ourselves to Him in faith, and though we struggle to work out our beliefs with consistency, our hearts are truly His. That internal confidence earned us the greatest reward: eternity with our Savior.

There's nothing wrong with having a healthy degree of self-confidence; in fact, building your faith may also build up your ability to think properly of yourself. But no matter how many social skills you develop, don't trust in them alone. Because everything they offer will be here today and gone in eternity. Only faith in Jesus lasts forever.

# GRACE AND PEACE

*Grace to you and peace from God our Father*
*and the Lord Jesus Christ.*
EPHESIANS 1:2 NKJV

First-century secular writers often wished the recipients of their mail grace and peace—it was a common greeting of the age. The apostle Paul picked up on this, but even from these few words, it's apparent the writer of many New Testament epistles gave it a new meaning. Can you imagine pagans connecting grace and peace with God the Father and Jesus? Though they may have been seeking peace in their lives, how distasteful Christianity would have been to many of them!

Paul used ideas common to the culture around him, not as an excuse to become like the pagans, but as a bridge to show others—Christian and non-Christian—what God was like. Perhaps some seeking the peace that eluded them found it through Paul's description of the grace and peace God freely offered. There's no question that Paul's epistles have had a powerful effect on people throughout history.

Today, the need for these two blessings has not lessened. Lives torn by doubt and fear still seek them. Paul's testimony can still reach people. But unless they see God working in the lives of believers, they're unlikely to put much stock in these words. It's so easy for those who have never met Jesus to discount His truths.

God has given us His grace and peace. Are we building bridges to those who need to experience them? Or have we walled ourselves inside a Christian tower, only meeting those who already show these qualities? Like Paul, we need to radiate God's truths and speak them with peace and grace to all who will hear.

# DEFINE SLOW

*The Lord is not slow in keeping his promise,*
*as some understand slowness. He is patient with you,*
*not wanting anyone to perish, but everyone to come to repentance.*
2 PETER 3:9

Time may drag as you're waiting for God to aid you in changing a bad habit or to bring newness to a difficult relationship. You begin to wonder if He'll ever intervene. Then when you least expect it, He brings wonderful change into your life. Was God slow? No, He just had another plan, and when the time was perfect, He did what you'd asked for.

It's the same, Peter told his readers, with the day of the Lord, the time when Jesus will return for His people. Because it hadn't happened on these first-century believers' schedule, they began to doubt the promise. When nonbelievers scoffed at their faith, the Christians asked, "Why is God so slow?"

Peter assured them God had not forgotten His people or His promise. He simply had a better plan—one that would add many others to the kingdom. As it turned out, Jesus didn't return during their century. But that doesn't mean He wasn't faithful. Though the early Christians might have been stunned that God would wait so long, they couldn't have argued with the need for many others to come to Him.

It's all a matter of how we define *slow*. If it means "anything that doesn't fit into our schedules," we *would* consider God slow. But if it means "something behind God's schedule," the word can't be used about God's plan. He's never behind on His own timetable. So, no, God isn't slow in coming—or in doing anything else in our lives. The real question is: "Are we on God's schedule or our own?"

# DEEP ROOTS

*Blessed is the man who. . .is like a tree planted by streams of water,*
*which yields its fruit in season and whose leaf does not wither.*
*Whatever he does prospers.*
PSALM 1:1, 3

What a delightful picture of a faithful person: a well-watered tree that never drops its leaves. It's easy to imagine a large tree, spreading wide and bearing plentifully. We'd like to be like that tree, sending our roots deep into life and finding a lot of prosperity.

So why don't Christians stand head and shoulders above other people in this world? Maybe it's because not many of us do what the rest of this psalm says—we don't avoid the wicked and their ways; we don't delight in God's Word. We don't feed our tree with the right things. Instead of giving it pure water from the Scriptures, we allow it to drink in lies. So it begins to lose a few leaves, and we ignore them, below our boughs. We settle for a little fruit, instead of a complete harvest.

That's not the way it has to be. It isn't what God designed for us. That's why He gave the psalmist this description, to challenge believers to be steadfast in their faith. None of us needs to settle for a second-best Christianity.

If we have been faithful, let us challenge ourselves to become more so. And if we doubt that God has made us prosper, let us consider what prosperity means. Are we looking for more money and a bigger car or deeper faithfulness to Him? Which will shine brighter in eternity—the polish on that car or a life that gleams for Him?

# GOD LIVES HERE

*Submit yourselves, then, to God. Resist the devil,*
*and he will flee from you.*
JAMES 4:7

"The devil may visit us, but God lives here." Mademoiselle Baptistine, a character in the novel *Les Misérables*, uses these words to describe her faith that God will protect her home. For the Christian, there's a lot of truth in her statement. When God lives inside us and controls our hearts and minds, the devil can only visit. We've taken part in a change of ownership that so brings God into our daily lives that His enemy makes no more than a brief temptation call on us, instead of sitting down in our parlor and making himself at home.

Do you know people who have walked down an aisle or listened to a Christian testimony, said they'd accepted Jesus, then never went to church or Bible study? They may have spoken the words of commitment, but have they invited God into the living room, kitchen, and bedroom of their lives? Probably not. Perhaps they'd figure they'd done a good thing if they let Him stay in the garage.

Having God live within us means He lives in all the rooms of our houses. No barriers go up when He wants to enter the bedroom because we've hidden items He wouldn't approve of there. No space in our homes remains a foothold of the devil's, a spot where he's more welcome than God.

We may struggle to let God into the den, but as we make a choice to open the door and offer Him our hospitality, the devil flees out the back door. Suddenly, God lives there, and evil no longer wants to remain.

# CRUSHED UNDERFOOT

*The God of peace will soon crush Satan under your feet.*
ROMANS 16:20

As the Romans faced division within the church, caused by false teaching, Paul gave them this promise: The God who had given them peace, through Jesus, would not desert them. As they continued to obey Him and avoid evil, Satan would be defeated. But obedience was critical to the success of this spiritual mission; God does not crush Satan under the feet of the disobedient.

Often, we don't feel Satan has been crushed under our feet. *Where is the power of God?* we may wonder. *Why hasn't He finished off Satan in our lives?* So we're tempted to become a little less faithful. *After all,* we ask ourselves, *does it really matter anyway?*

As we ask that question, Satan, who would like to see us become less than faithful, has already impacted our lives. We lose spiritual consistency, and the door opens for him. Instead of walking *on* Satan, we're walking *with* him. It doesn't take long for us to slide in Bible study, church attendance, and the other spiritual disciplines that keep us faithful. Soon our actions slip, too.

But when we remain faithful—though we haven't seen the evil one between our toes—and trust that God will keep His promises, God begins to work. Small changes in our spiritual lives may have larger ones in His kingdom, as we stand firm in the faith Paul shared with the Romans. Unexpectedly, we may find someone we witnessed to long ago has come to the Lord, or a Christian friend who struggled with sin has turned again to Jesus. And in the end, when we reach heaven, we'll clearly see the impact of faithfulness, as Satan is overcome entirely.

# SATISFIED SOULS

*May God himself, the God of peace, sanctify you through and through.*
*May your whole spirit, soul and body be kept blameless*
*at the coming of our Lord Jesus Christ.*
1 THESSALONIANS 5:23

Ah, this is the picture of a satisfied soul. Made holy through and through, the believer rests in Jesus. That Christian can look forward to standing before God, satisfied that every necessary mission is accomplished.

It's not by chance that Paul puts this comment at the end of 1 Thessalonians. He's already shared his message describing how the Christians of Thessalonica can obey God. He's written about the Lord's coming, given instructions on Christian living, and warned them to avoid evil. But Paul isn't promising them a future sitting on their laurels, doing nothing but singing psalms. God's battle against evil has only begun. Paul asks that He will continue to make them holy, through whatever challenges lie ahead. Knowing God will be faithful to all His people, Paul looks past the challenges believers face on earth to the final outcome of faith.

We might like to think Christianity has more hours of laurel sitting than battle. None of us prefers hard work to the blessings of peace, yet we can't have one without the other. God's sanctification is worked out in our lives with effort, and no one achieves spiritual growth only by singing psalms. That restful part of our lives blesses us between the battles that put sin in its proper place—behind us.

One day, we won't have to settle for brief spells of satisfaction. We'll spend all eternity singing God's praises for the victories He gave us on earth. Our mission accomplished, we'll fill heaven with the rejoicing of satisfied souls.

# AWESOME DEEDS

*You faithfully answer our prayers with awesome deeds,*
*O God our savior. You are the hope of everyone on earth.*
PSALM 65:5 NLT

Prayer life feeling a little lackluster? Then read this verse. Mull it over a bit and trust that God really means what He says. Awesome deeds? In response to our prayers? Why don't we frequently receive responses like that? Maybe we'd better take another look at this praying thing.

Obviously, when we hope for an awesome response to our communication with God, it's not because we're so wonderful. Finding the perfect way to ask won't work—that's expecting magic, not faith. But somehow, as we do ordinary petitioning, God provides the wonderful answers.

David doesn't talk much, in this psalm, about the qualities of himself, the prayer. Instead he is simply lost in awe at how wonderful the Lord is, and that's the right focus for prayer. As long as we puff ourselves up, talk to God about how wonderful we are or all the plans we have for our spiritual lives, our faith goes nowhere. We were never meant to be the focus of prayer. Our petty concerns pale beside the abilities and plans of our heavenly Father, who made heaven, earth, and even us. Unworshipful prayer may feel good to us, but it simply hits the ceiling. No wonder we don't get much response.

But when we treat God as if He really is our hope on earth, praise Him for His wonderful deeds, and worship Him, the awesome deeds can start—the change in us is only the beginning!

# SECOND TIME AROUND

*Then the word of the LORD came to Jonah a second time:*
*"Go to the great city of Nineveh*
*and proclaim to it the message I give you."*
JONAH 3:1–2

Does God have to tell you a second time, like Jonah, or do you listen when He first asks you to take on a difficult task for Him?

It's not hard to understand Jonah's refusal. God wanted to send His prophet to the capital of Assyria, Israel's enemy. This extremely violent nation, expert at wiping out other countries, was the war machine of the day, and other countries feared it for good reason. They were not nice people. But Jonah knew his compassionate God and feared that instead of punishing the wicked Assyrians, He would forgive them. Preferring his enemies in hell, the prophet refused to do God's command.

*What was Jonah thinking?* we ask ourselves. *Didn't he know God's in control of everything, and if He wants people saved, they will be?* It's so easy to see the story clearly when it's from another person's perspective. But we've done it ourselves, haven't we? God asks us to speak to a person about Him, and we keep putting it off. We'll do it "someday." He asks us to begin a ministry, and we resist, figuring we're not "spiritual" enough.

When we respond that way, like Jonah, we may end up in a painful situation. We probably won't enter a fish's belly, but hurt can still find us for awhile. In the end, God will bring us to do His will after all. He gives a second chance, and we'll obey this time—unless we prefer sitting in the twenty-first century equivalent of a fish belly.

# WORDS INTO WORKS

*"I am the LORD your God,*
*who brought you out of the land of Egypt,*
*out of the house of bondage."*
EXODUS 20:2 NKJV

At first, when my pastor began reading the Ten Commandments at every Sunday-morning service, I expected it to be dull. A few weeks later, as I listened again, I reminded myself that few people—even few Christians—can reproduce these commandments with any accuracy. Sure, we know them vaguely, and we might even begin to live by them, but we lack the focus that makes them a powerful part of our lives.

It's not hard to take well-known Scriptures lightly. Sure we've heard and read them. We might even be able to rattle them off quickly. But the Bible wasn't meant to become familiar to us—it was meant to change our lives.

When God spoke this verse, through Moses, He wasn't telling the Israelites anything they didn't already know. It wasn't all that long after the spectacular exodus. But instead of searching for God, His people had begun searching for a better life—one that gave them better things and an easier lifestyle.

So He reminded them of being in Egypt, where they had no freedom and were often abused by their masters. Then, to improve their focus, He gave them the life-changing commandments that told them so much about Him and all of life's relationships. It was up to them whether to listen or ignore what God had to say, but their decision would make a big change in their lives.

That's why I'm listening carefully each Sunday, to put these words into works in my life. I want my focus to be on all He's already done and what He wants to do in my life.

# END-TIMES PLAN

*The end of the world is coming soon.*
*Therefore, be earnest and disciplined in your prayers.*
1 PETER 4:7 NLT

You've seen the cartoons showing a strange-looking person walking down a street, carrying a sign announcing the imminent end of the world. You might never do that, but if you knew the end was near, what would you do? Would you knock on your neighbors' doors and try to drag them into the kingdom in the short time at your command? Would you stand on the steps of a public place, witnessing to any whom you could collar?

Neither is what Peter would have done—or what he commands us to do. Instead he tells his readers to pray. And because Scripture is clear that we are in the last age (Hebrews 9:26; 1 John 2:18), the apostle wasn't just speaking hypothetically.

*So, the world is falling part, and we're supposed to take part in a prayer meeting?* you many wonder. Yes. Not that we're *only* supposed to pray, but as in all things, our relationship to Jesus is the most important part of our lives. As evangelicals, we say we base everything on Him. So wouldn't we want His input on how to handle this critical part of history? Don't we want to do His will down to our very last hour?

We know the power of prayer. What greater need could we have, than to have God guide our steps as we near the end of history? With His impact on our lives, whether He tarries one day or a thousand years, we are ready.

Now is the time for real, disciplined prayer. Is it part of our end-times plan?

# COVERED WITH SACKCLOTH?

*"But let man and beast be covered with sackcloth.*
*Let everyone call urgently on God.*
*Let them give up their evil ways and their violence."*
JONAH 3:8

The Assyrians had a lot to repent for. When this violent, wicked people heard about their upcoming destruction by God, Jonah's words hit their hearts. They couldn't seem to ask forgiveness fast enough. Their king demanded that even the beasts be covered with sackcloth, a rough, uncomfortable fabric that indicated repentance.

I don't know about your animals, but I certainly doubt my basset hounds' ability to repent. When I catch one of them in wrongdoing, I get that mournful look many people mistake for "feeling sorry," but I'm not fooled. I know that if they're sorry, it's because they got caught, not because they have some finer moral feeling. Chances are that I will catch that hound in the same kind of act within the next week—if not the next day! Getting an animal to "repent" and change actions is more a matter of training than appealing to a higher moral code.

Why did the king cover animals in sackcloth? Because he was trying to show a total repentance that might encourage God to forgive them. The king wanted nothing between his nation and God's mercy.

We don't cover our cats and dogs in sackcloth or make a new covering for the bird's cage. Because we appreciate God's generous mercy, we know He's not going to blame our animals or wipe us out because they didn't appear properly repentant. But do we also appreciate the mercy that saved us from as much destruction as the Assyrians? Do we feel the joyful thanks of those ancient people and live in a way that shows our appreciation?

If not, maybe we'd better search out sackcloth for our hearts.

# PASS IT ON

*One generation shall praise Your works to another,*
*And shall declare Your mighty acts.*

PSALM 145:4 NASB

God's works are so wonderful, the excited Christian can hardly contain them. When a believer's on fire for Jesus, it's hard not to share that news with others. Young Christians especially seem unable to stop telling the good news about Jesus. Though they may offend some folks as they tell their story, they get the message out.

As time goes on, that flame doesn't burn as brightly. We grow older in the Lord, and instead of being like a newly started fire, we burn a little lower. Though we still provide warmth and light, we're a bit more under control. That's part of growing in the Lord, and it's good, but it shouldn't keep us from finding a way to tell others about Jesus. Maybe we won't witness to our families at every juncture, but we wisely choose opportunities to meet their needs and tell of our love for God.

No matter how old we get in the Lord, He provides us with ways to share our faith. Whether it's in family devotional time or just a moment when we tell our children how faithful God has been in a situation, we have a story to share. Sometimes our excitement blazes high, and at others it burns a little lower, but whether or not we have children, we always need to pass on the story. How will they know, if we never open our mouths and share the praise God put on our hearts?

# ABUNDANT LIFE

*"The thief comes only to steal and kill and destroy;*
*I came that they may have life, and have it abundantly."*
JOHN 10:10 NASB

Abundant life, full of good things on this earth, spiritual peace and joy, and full, satisfying relationships—that's what God intends His people to have. But listen to the world, and you'd never know it. Non-Christians often portray Christians as narrow-minded, sad, or hopelessly idealistic.

That's probably not the faith you know. Because Jesus entered your life, you've entered a new realm—and it's not the Twilight Zone, either. Life has taken on a new meaning, because you know the Creator. You feel clean, right with your Maker, and richer for being in a relationship with Him. Though you're far from perfect, He's been working in your life to bring spiritual abundance, deeper understanding of Him and the world around you, and a joy that doesn't stop when trouble enters the door.

Nonbelievers can't know any of that. You can tell them that loving Jesus is the best thing ever, and they'll wonder if you're zany. They've never experienced anything like it, so they can't imagine such peace and joy. And whatever we've never felt for ourselves, we humans tend to doubt.

But one day the thief who came to steal, kill, and destroy their lives makes them so miserable that God's message enters a crack in their armor against Him. They start to listen to His message of abundant life, and before long faith blossoms, breaking open the hardware that kept abundance at bay. New life, abundant life, takes hold.

It's time to rejoice in Jesus.

# CLEAR VISION

*Now we see but a poor reflection as in a mirror;*
*then we shall see face to face.*
*Now I know in part; then I shall know fully,*
*even as I am fully known.*
1 CORINTHIANS 13:12

I came to know Jesus," we often say. It's a common Christian expression, one that might imply to some that we have a corner on the market of God. They could think we believe there's nothing more to Him than we have in our minds and spirits.

Yet even Paul, a spiritual giant, didn't think he had it all together when it came to knowing Jesus. Though he'd preached the gospel across much of the world and he knew and had studied the Old Testament for years, he compared his understanding of God to a reflection in a mirror—and not a very good one, at that. Paul tells us he has a little knowledge of Jesus. God is so much larger than any of us can imagine.

But one day, each Christian shall have a different relationship with the Lord. There will be no gaps of knowledge. Every believer will know Jesus thoroughly, just as He now knows each of us. We'll be able to fully comprehend the magnitude of our Savior.

While we're here on earth, we still need to polish up that mirror and see as clearly as we can who God is and what He desires of us. But someday, we know we can look forward to not having to think about what God might want—it will be as clear as looking through glass, not peering into some clouded mirror. Then, we'll *really* know Jesus.

# WHAT'S IN A NAME?

*"Until now you have not asked for anything in my name.*
*Ask and you will receive, and your joy will be complete."*
JOHN 16:24

Has anyone ever asked anything in your name? Perhaps your child invoked your name when seeking help from one of your friends, "I'm Terry Smith's daughter," or "I'm Kathy Moore's son." Chances are, your friend was quickly ready to help. Because that person knew you, your child was important.

It's the same when we go to God and pray in Jesus' name. God recognizes that we have received His forgiveness, through His Son, and He's happy to grant us our wishes. He gives good things that make us happy.

But that doesn't mean He gives us everything we ask for. If your child tried to borrow a million dollars from your friend, and your friend knew your credit didn't run that high, no money would be forthcoming. The request wouldn't be like you—wouldn't fit with your personality and abilities. Just so, the requests we place before God have to "look" like Jesus. If we ask for something that isn't part of Him—if it's a selfish request, or aimed at wrongdoing—we won't get it.

But when we ask in Jesus' will—for an ailing friend who needs healing, a relative who doesn't have salvation and is desperately seeking, or our own spiritual growth—God is happy to give. Only instead of looking just the way we expect, our answer may take a different form. That's because all of our answers have to look just like Jesus.

# GOOD GIFT?

*"If you then, being evil, know how to give good gifts to your children,*
*how much more will your Father who is in heaven*
*give good things to those who ask Him!"*
MATTHEW 7:11 NKJV

Ever wonder if the things God was giving you were all good? As you faced a trial, perhaps you wanted to know what He had in mind. Or maybe your child came home with a trouble, while you were in the middle of another crisis, and you wondered, *Why me, Lord?*

It's not unusual for us to question our trials. If we went out looking for troubles, we'd be sadists—naturally we'd prefer to avoid all the problems we can. Sensibly we make efforts to make our lives smooth and prosperous.

So when we've been praying faithfully, seeking God's will, and trying our best, but trouble still afflicts us, maybe it isn't all evil. Instead, God might have a blessing that can only come when we've been tested. That struggling child may need attention during his challenging situation, but it may become the key to a better relationship.

Even in the midst of our worst troubles, we can trust that, as Jesus said, God still remembers how to give good gifts. Though we don't like our situations, God's ability to give good things hasn't dried up. And as we cannot forget our children, how much less can He erase our relationship from His memory.

If we, who lack all God's powers, do good things for those we love, how much more is He willing to do them for us? All we need do is trust that something good lies at the end of this trial—something God had in mind for us all along.

# THE BEST NEWS

*"At last the time has come!" he announced. "The Kingdom of God is near!*
*Turn from your sins and believe this Good News!"*
MARK 1:15 NLT

What a funny place to find good news—at the end of repentance. We tend to think of repentance as a difficult thing, and often it is, as we struggle to see the world from God's point of view. The sin that holds on to a deep part of our beings is not easily eradicated. No, repentance is not fun or easy.

But let's remember no really good things come easily. We struggle to develop good careers and build good family lives. Yet we expect God's Good News—the best thing in all the world—not to demand much of us.

The benefit of coming to Jesus and accepting His salvation is huge. From sin that entraps us so we cannot escape, He frees us in a moment of simple faith. But God's good things aren't magic. They don't free us from consequences and make us shallow people who expect to do whatever we want and still receive a blessing. God wants to build us up in character and make us just like Him.

So while the Good News is simple, free to all who accept it, and priceless, it isn't without cost. Jesus paid His life to offer us freedom from sin, and He expects us to take that gift seriously.

Take hold of this good gift God has for you. Accept the bad news that you've sinned, and offer that wrong up to Him. He'll reply with the Good News that Jesus died for it all, and your repentance has already given you the best His kingdom has to offer: forgiveness for every sin.

# ALL GOOD

*For everything God created is good,*
*and nothing is to be rejected if it is received with thanksgiving.*
1 TIMOTHY 4:4

God didn't create anything that wasn't good, Paul stated emphatically in the face of heretical teachers who wanted to deny Christians everything from marriage to meat. The apostle made it clear that God didn't tease us by putting extra temptations in the world—denying us the best it had to offer.

Has God given you good things? In our culture, that often implies a huge house, a fancy car, and steak for dinner. But haven't you had a house you loved, even though it wasn't in the finest part of town, an older car you didn't want to get rid of, or a macaroni-and-cheese dinner that fed your stomach and your tastebuds as well as any steak? Good things don't have to cost a lot of money.

Your best relationships are priceless. Would you trade a much-loved parent for money or a spouse for gold? These too are gifts from the heavenly Father, who knows how to give the best—no matter the cost.

And what of the other things God creates that have no price? A sunset filled with vibrant colors, a nighttime sky that shades from light to darkest blue and is sprinkled with glowing stars, a drink of water that quenches thirst as no man-made beverage can. God has given generously, in many more ways than we often consider.

But no matter what God gives us, whether it's a no-frills economy car or a luxury coupe, a filet mignon or chicken, we are to receive it with thanks. He made it just for us, and we're enjoying the benefit, so why not share that joy with Jesus? He's the best gift God had to offer—and we didn't reject it, either.

# FREE INDEED!

*Through Christ Jesus the law of the Spirit of life*
*set me free from the law of sin and death.*
ROMANS 8:2

Have you struggled with sin, feeling you could never win over it? The apostle Paul had that same experience. Romans 7 describes his struggle to do right. But the harder He tried, the more frustrated he became, and the more impossible it felt.

The battle seemed impossible, because it was. In our own strength, we will always give in to sin, no matter how hard we try to resist. While we're vigilant at the front door, Satan sneaks in the back. Trying hard simply isn't the solution, because rules and regulations can't keep us from wrong thoughts and actions. It didn't work for Paul, who knew all the Old Testament commandments, and it won't work for us, even if we memorize the whole Bible. When we try to be good that way, we're simply relying on our own weak abilities.

But that doesn't mean there isn't a solution. Though we can't extract ourselves from sin, God can. When all our best efforts fail, we need to ask ourselves how we became free in the first place. When we gave ourselves to Him, God's grace freed us. The Spirit of life liberated us from sin, only through our faith in Jesus.

The solution that worked in the first moment we trusted Jesus works when we face sin today. We can still throw ourselves entirely on Him, asking Him to release us from temptations. As we place ourselves completely in His hands, much as we did when we first believed, His Spirit takes control of our lives and blesses us with the freedom we've been seeking all along. Then we are free indeed!

# EXCELLENT THINGS

*"Sing to the LORD,*
*For He has done excellent things;*
*This is known in all the earth."*
ISAIAH 12:5 NKJV

Excellent things! God doesn't just do good things or the best things. He does excellent things. What could improve on God's superb plan or will? But do we appreciate what He has done for us?

This verse comes from a prophetic praise that looks forward to the day of the Lord. In the return of the Messiah, when the Israelites see their salvation, Isaiah promises they will appreciate the excellent things He has done for them. The doubts they had here on earth will all be swept away as they understand and praise Him.

But God had already done many wonderful things for His people—they had been brought out of bondage and into the Promised Land, and He'd made Israel great under King David. But when they became unfaithful, they fell into weakness, and the Assyrians overcame their small country. No longer could they appreciate God's excellence and all He'd done for them. Blinded by sin to His greatness, most could not appreciate Him. Only a few remaining faithful ones were left to claim that God was still doing excellent things.

Are our eyes open to the excellent things He's done for His people—and is still doing for them today? We have seen the fulfillment of the Messianic prophecies that precede this verse and felt the impact of His salvation. We know much that was hidden to the ancient Israelites. Yet sin can blind our eyes, too.

Have we thanked God for the excellent things of the past and present? Are we looking forward to the joys of the future? Have we truly appreciated Him in prayer and praise?

# PRAYER POWER

*He is also able to save to the uttermost*
*those who come to God through Him,*
*since He always lives to make intercession for them.*
HEBREWS 7:25 NKJV

Have you ever gotten tired of intercessory prayer? The person you prayed for didn't seem to "get it." That prayer didn't seem to go farther than the ceiling, after you'd prayed for a month, a year, or even longer. Perhaps you put that prayer on the back burner or gave up altogether.

If you need a new view of the importance of your prayers, take a look at this verse. Jesus never stops interceding for us—He's always before the Father, bringing important issues before Him and asking Him to work in our behalf. You might say that as our High Priest His mission is our salvation—one He doesn't forget or become tired of pursuing. Prayer is part of that mission to save us completely.

Unlike Jesus, we don't have that kind of forever ministry. People can't say we will always be able to intercede for their worldly woes. The time we have to ask Him to save a loved one, work out a problem, or intervene in an international crisis is limited to the few years we have on this earth. But by placing us in this world, God's given us a mission, too, and prayer is part of it. By lifting others up to Him, we take part in the blessing He bestows on our world.

Just as Jesus won't forget us, we need to remember those whose lives we touch. Because we know Jesus, we can pray effectively—and perhaps that's the most potent impact we'll have on another's life.

# SNAKE TAIL

*Then the LORD said to him,*
*"Reach out your hand and take it by the tail."*
*So Moses reached out and took hold of the snake*
*and it turned back into a staff in his hand.*

EXODUS 4:4

When I was in grammar school, a student brought a pet snake into class to show it off. The trouble started when another student, unfamiliar with snakes, tried to pick it up. Had he known about serpents, he'd have grabbed it just behind the head, but this innocent grabbed it farther back and got bitten for his curiosity. A whole lot of hoopla followed.

Anyone who knows snakes knows you don't pick them up by the tail, because they can reach around and bite you. Living in the ancient world, Moses probably knew that. So when God commanded him to grab that reptile by the tail, he probably felt a moment of horror. But there was something worse—would Moses disobey the Lord and leave it on the ground or grab it at another part of its anatomy? Wisely, the prophet did as God commanded, and it all turned out right, as the snake turned back into his staff.

Has God asked you to do something scary? As Moses might have, you may wonder for a second if He really means what He says. "What? The tail, Lord?" the prophet might have asked. But in a second he probably remembered he was talking to the Lord of the universe, who knew all about snake tails. The prophet could hardly tell the Creator something new, just as you cannot tell God something He hasn't considered.

Remember, if God asks you to take a snake by the tail, He also knows He plans to turn it into a rod. You're completely safe.

# GOD'S FRIEND

*"But you, O Israel, my servant, Jacob, whom I have chosen,*
*you descendants of Abraham my friend,*
*I took you from the ends of the earth,*
*from its farthest corners I called you.*
*I said, 'You are my servant';*
*I have chosen you and have not rejected you."*

ISAIAH 41:8–9

Have you pondered the idea that, like Israel, the Lord of the universe is your friend? Perhaps you've been stopped in your tracks by the awe of that truth. *Why should He care for me?* you may wonder.

God chooses His friends on His own terms. The famous, the extraordinarily intelligent, the powerful aren't always on His list. Yet some of the most unexpected folks are. He doesn't choose based on worldly greatness (He doesn't need it, because He has enough greatness of His own). His own sense of mercy defines the choice, in ways we cannot now understand.

Many blessings follow friendship with God, but so do challenges. The Creator expects much of His friends, just as He gives much. He doesn't ask just anyone to take on the job, which also requires training in faithfulness. Anyone not willing to do His will need not apply for the position. Being a friend of Jesus requires that we suffer, struggle, and face numerous challenges, physically and spiritually. It's not the kind of thing He offers lightly or we should accept blindly.

But when God chooses a friend, it's forever. He never gives up or changes His mind. He's with you for this lifetime and eternity. Along with all the purely delightful things in His hand, He offers strength in trials and guidance for a long, hard way. Nothing that happens is beyond His strength or help.

That's the best friendship anyone could offer.

# TOTAL BLESSING

*Dear friend, I pray that you may enjoy good health and that*
*all may go well with you, even as your soul is getting along well.*
3 JOHN 2

When the apostle John wrote his friend Gaius, he not only wished spiritual blessings on him, but prayed that his health and his life would go well, too.

It's so easy for us to become so spiritually minded that we forget people's other needs. Because we know faith is the most important thing, we pray for a friend's spiritual condition, but do we also pray that physical needs would be met? Do we ask God to help the new widow financially and emotionally, as well as spiritually? Or do we see that as the responsibility of others? Even if we know she doesn't know Jesus, do we reach out in concrete love that can touch her life in other ways?

God's blessings begin with the spiritual, but they don't end there. We've often had reason to praise Him because He brought us enough money for the rent or mortgage payment when we didn't know where it would come from. He's given us good health, after we visited the doctor's office and began to fear the worst. He's answered our prayers for another church member to be healed.

Just as God recognizes the needs of this world, we should, too. We can't separate the body from the soul, and often it's the body's needs that make people aware of a spiritual emptiness. God deals with every phase of our lives, and as we offer Jesus to others, we can do that, too.

Then they can learn what it means to be totally blessed.

# FLYAWAY BLESSINGS

*Cast but a glance at riches, and they are gone,*
*for they will surely sprout wings and fly off to the sky like an eagle.*
PROVERBS 23:5

Ever hear the secular version of this proverb? It says, "Money talks. It says good-bye." Even those who don't know God can't miss the fact that money is far from permanent. With that knowledge, it's amazing people put so much trust in it. Yet some will do wrong or put their relationships with God and others in jeopardy just to get more of this flying material.

God tells us not to trust in riches for a reason. They may make us feel secure, but that feeling is just a myth. At the very moment we feel nothing can touch us, we're in danger. We've given ourselves over to an idol, because anything that draws us away from God can be called that.

A greater, better security has nothing to do with a bank account, secure job, or any of the things we tend to trust in. Anyone who has faithfully suffered through a time of unemployment or financial loss knows this security. No matter what is forfeited, God remains faithful. Whether war, death of a loved one, or financial ruin stare the believer in the face, the Rock, Jesus Christ, remains firm. While money and riches fly away like an eagle, Jesus remains, no matter what happens on this side of heaven. When life is over, the best blessing is still to come—an eternity praising the One who never fails.

God doesn't expect His people to trust in flyaway blessings, when they can have the very best. He offers Himself as security for this life and eternity. Why would anyone choose anything less?

# PLEASURABLE DAYS

*Remember now your Creator in the days of your youth,*
*Before the difficult days come,*
*And the years draw near when you say,*
*"I have no pleasure in them."*
ECCLESIASTES 12:1 NKJV

Good news! You don't have to wait until you're old and gray to come to God and receive His blessings. He wants even young people to accept Him. No one can say that you are too young to know Jesus. In fact, statistics show that most people come to Him by age eighteen. God loves young people.

Maybe that's partly because He doesn't want to see people suffer unnecessarily. Instead of leaving them to work out their lives in their own ways, fall into sin, and make a mess of things, He wants to guide them in the choice of a mate, a career, and a lifestyle. He wants to shower many blessings on them for a lifetime, instead of limiting His impact to a few years. As He touches their lives early, He knows they will have better, more enjoyable lives—and lives that glorify Him longer.

You don't have to be facing the end of your life to be blessed by Jesus. He wants to bless you today. Whether you are under eighteen, just over it, or several decades beyond, He wants to share His love for as many years as you'll let Him.

Before sin has squeezed the pleasure from your days, trouble has furrowed your brow, and your relationships seem more trouble than they're worth, turn to Jesus. When you face difficult days, as all people do, you won't stand alone. Trouble won't blast your life but will strengthen you instead. Your Creator can turn all trials to blessings, if you just stand firm in Him.

Enjoy your days in Jesus.

# LOVE LIFE

*The LORD is far from the wicked,*
*But He hears the prayer of the righteous.*
PROVERBS 15:29 NKJV

From one year to another, a man who doesn't love God doesn't pray, until a loved one becomes ill. Then the desperate unbeliever may decide to give prayer a try. But if God doesn't respond "properly," by saving the ill one, he complains God doesn't exist or doesn't care about people.

What that weak prayer doesn't understand is that God doesn't have to respond to every petition. Praying is part of an intimate relation with Him, and anyone who attempts to ask for blessings apart from that relationship is coming to a complete stranger and asking for great wealth. Trading on the good will of someone you don't know is a risky business, and in this context, it's not one God encourages.

Yet the one who does not know Him is not entirely without hope. Jesus calls people to come to Him in repentance. The woman in trouble who admits her need of the Savior suddenly realizes that God does answer prayer. Though He may not respond the way she expected, great blessing can follow, even in the midst of terrible trial.

God loves to listen to His people, and when have you heard a Christian complain about having prayed too much? In a deep, caring relationship, neither party can speak too much to the other. Just as a man and woman who have newly discovered love discuss all their joys and cares, the Christian shares everything with the Lord.

Has prayer become mechanical, a chore instead of a joy? Remember how beloved you are by the One you're speaking to. He doesn't want to hear the details of just anyone's life—He's asked you to share with Him, and you're blessed to know His love.

# SILVER-TONGUED SAINT

*The tongue of the righteous is as choice silver,*
*The heart of the wicked is worth little.*
PROVERBS 10:20 NASB

Going faithfully about our daily lives, we may not think we have a great impact on our world for Jesus. We can try to live honestly, do a good job, and raise our families well, but the day-to-day business of our lives seems so small. What importance do they have in the great scheme of things?

God doesn't say we all have to be spiritual giants. Not every Christian will be a Mother Teresa or a Billy Graham. We may not reach around the world to people, unless it's with our missions giving. But that doesn't mean God doesn't value all we do.

This proverb describes a basic difference between the faithful believer and the unbeliever. When Christians speak out, wherever they are, using the wisdom of the Scriptures, their words become important. They may not get the public attention that one wicked opinion maker who's covered with approbation by the media receives, but to God, their faithfulness is worth more than any TV or radio coverage. Though each believer may only touch a few lives, that impact may go far beyond any famous person's reach.

Clearly, we need to understand that though God can use politicians or radio or television personalities to accomplish His will, He doesn't have to. Public opinion doesn't have to go with Him, and it rarely does.

But in the end, when the final day of justice comes, God may show the whole world that the blessed silver-tongued saint who lived down the street was priceless to Him and His work, while the wicked opinion maker was nearly valueless to anyone.

# FROM CRAWLING TO WALKING

*"God is my strength and power,*
*And He makes my way perfect."*
2 SAMUEL 22:33 NKJV

Many Christians, when they first come to the Lord, have a surge of spiritual fervor. So thoroughly changed is life that they seem to soar into faith easily. Not unexpectedly, they think this is the way Christianity will always be. Nothing should overtake them.

Perhaps that happens because the new Christian has nothing but Jesus to depend on. The church isn't more important than God, and man-made doctrines have yet to impact the baby Christian. Life seems so good, and the baby doesn't know that this isn't Christian maturity, but a blessing God gives to His infants.

But when that infant begins to crawl into the Christian life, suddenly everything may become a struggle. What seemed so easy has become difficult. Sins that once apparently had no impact are daily frustrations. What happened?

Like a growing child, the Christian begins to face challenges that cause growth. Spiritual muscles must develop, and that only happens when they're flexed. If God made faith easy forever, He'd only have a series of cribs with stunted babes in them.

As those challenges come, some of them difficult and long, the believer starts to realize nothing can be done in human power. God is the only strength and power behind faith—without Him there is just hardship, and perfection remains elusive.

As the walk of faith becomes harder, only trusting in Jesus alone allows a Christian to joyously walk that straight and narrow way. But what delight it is to walk with Him for the rest of life!

# ON HIGH PLACES

*"He [God] makes my feet like the feet of deer,*
*And sets me on my high places."*
2 SAMUEL 22:34 NKJV

L ike a bounding deer, the believer who trusts in God jumps from
rock to rock, unfazed by the hardness underfoot. What a lovely
image David gave us in this psalm describing the blessings God offers
to those who trust entirely in Him.

*If only we could trust God perfectly each day and rise constantly up,*
*higher on the mountain,* we decide. We'd like to think that's an ideal
Christian experience. But our spiritual landscape does not consist simply of mountains. Valleys lie between the uplands, as David attested
when he wrote: "Even though I walk through the valley of the shadow
of death" (Psalm 23:4). And without those valleys, there would be no
mountains at all.

All believers, spiritual giants like David or those of more average
size, cannot forever rise above trouble. Until we live in a heavenly
world, a fallen world's hardships impact us. However, whether we set
our feet on high places or valleys, one thing remains the same. When
David wrote about God's blessing in helping us overcome trouble or
about the joy of completed overcoming, he realized one truth.
Challenges that threaten to undo us or joy at overcoming share one
thing: God never leaves us in either situation. "I will fear no evil, for
you are with me," Psalm 23:4 continues. And 2 Samuel 22:51 con-
cludes, " 'He gives his king great victories.' "

So whether we're bounding along in faith, or struggling through
a doleful valley, our faith does not change. We still trust in the One
who made both mountains and valleys, and He'll faithfully see us
through either.

# REST FOR THE WEARY

*The LORD replied, "My Presence will go with you,*
*and I will give you rest."*
EXODUS 33:14

L abor comes in so many varieties. We labor to bring in an income, to pray daily and study the Word, to meet the spiritual needs of others, and to be good parents, children, or grandparents. Often we feel overwhelmed by all we must accomplish in a day.

When we feel that way, there is a solution—as He did for Moses, God offers to take up our burdens and give us much-needed relief. As we simply cling to this promise, He gives us rest.

But it's up to us to go to the Lord with our needs. Often we get so caught up in trying to find our own solutions, we simply don't tell Him about them. It's as if we assume He knows, so we need not talk about it. But we forget that God doesn't barge into our lives. As long as we hold on to finding our own solutions to what overwhelms us, He'll let us lose our way in our own efforts.

If we take advantage of His offer and come to Him, everything changes. As we ask God for help, He lifts all our burdens, and where once we struggled, we experience His Spirit pulsing through our lives. When we place a trouble in God's hands, then take His advice, seemingly insolvable problems slip away or are lightened by our sharing them with the Savior. It's not magic, but a sweet release.

Working hard on our own, we create only stress, worry, and more uncertainty. Only resting in Him brings the answer to every need.

# AWED!

*Great is the LORD and most worthy of praise;*
*his greatness no one can fathom.*
PSALM 145:3

If you've ever tried to follow a man-made philosophy, you've discovered its limitations. As time went on, you found problems it couldn't solve or simply ignored because it had no answers. Even the "best" people can only take on so many issues—in their own power they can only do so much. Their greatness only goes so far.

But that's not true of God. No matter how many issues we bring to Him, He has an answer. No matter how low our lives seem to go, He can bring us up again. We see His hand at work in the nations or the minutia of our lives, and in both He remains faithful. Nothing lies beyond His grasp.

We may pride ourselves on being "scientific people," but what we call science is simply our understanding of His creation. We only comprehend a small part of His inventive mind. Despite centuries of study, we've just scratched the very surface of the world He made to share with us.

As we look at God's greatness and experience His love, awe fills our beings. Our scant ability to appreciate His personality and power lays bare our own smallness. Yet when the Creator points out their frailty to His faithful ones, He's not belittling us. He simply shares the truth of His own character. He reminds us that He also wants to share all He has and all He is with us. Instead of hoarding all He is and making us pay the price for our own weakness, He mercifully sent His Son to share all with us.

Could anything be greater or so deserve our awed praise?

# TOO HARD?

*"Is anything too hard for the LORD?*
*I will return to you at the appointed time next year*
*and Sarah will have a son."*
GENESIS 18:14

I s there something in your life that seems too hard even for God to deal with? A relationship turned sour, a work-related situation, a financial trouble? You've asked God for a solution, and it hasn't appeared quickly. So maybe, like Abraham and Sarah, you've been looking elsewhere for the answers.

God had promised this elderly couple a son. The idea thrilled them—an heir to take over the family business after Abraham died, a child to fill the empty arms of Sarah, who had struggled with barrenness. But time went on, and no son appeared, so they took matters into their own hands and tried to make this child of promise. Hagar, Sarah's servant, bore Abraham's son. But Ishmael still wasn't the child God promised. Tension filled their camp, instead of the peace that follows God's will.

Though the people weren't faithful, God was. They tried to do things their way, but it didn't change His promise. God wanted them to have a blessing, so He still sent the promised son, Isaac.

It's the same with the people He blesses today. We may decide a situation's impossible, run into trouble, and forget God. But He doesn't forget us. He still wants to bless us, and He will, but perhaps He has to get our attention first. As long as we're heading in the opposite direction, even if we received a blessing, we wouldn't appreciate it. Even the best God could give would become mired in our disobedience.

God wants to bless you today. Are you ready to receive all the good He has to offer?

# JESUS CARES

*O LORD, be gracious to us; we long for you.*
*Be our strength every morning, our salvation in time of distress.*
ISAIAH 33:2

Need strength? Require help? They're not far from you. Look no farther than your Savior. No matter what's going on in your life, He's always there, waiting for you to turn to Him.

Unlike Isaiah's contemporaries, you may not be facing overwhelming armies, ready to take your country hostage, but your daily challenges are still important to Jesus. Like the prophet, you can call on Him, no matter what you face. In fact, God tells you to share all your troubles with Him, because He cares for you (1 Peter 5:7). That means He's concerned about all the things you face, day by day, all the trials and troubles, everything that impacts your life.

On that tired morning, when it's hard to get moving, you can call on Jesus. When a life-changing problem looms ahead in your day, He cares about that, too. Can you find a problem He won't share with you or tells you to take somewhere else? No. He told you to give Him all your troubles, and He means just that. Whether it's a son or daughter who's hard to handle, a difficulty on the job, or a spiritual issue you can't seem to resolve, He offers both a listening ear and answers.

Do you long for help from God? Your desire is in the right place. Just ask, then trust He will answer. Tomorrow may not solve every problem, but you can know that help *is* on the way. You've put your faith in the eternal God who never fails. Talk to Him this morning, and watch help appear.

# A LISTENING EAR

*I love the LORD, for he heard my voice;*
*he heard my cry for mercy.*
*Because he turned his ear to me,*
*I will call on him as long as I live.*

PSALM 116:1–2

Have you known God listened to you? If you're a Christian, your answer has to be yes—God heard when you asked forgiveness for your sins and requested that He control your life. Like the psalmist, He saved you because you cried out for mercy.

But He didn't end His listening with salvation. That was only the beginning. From that moment, He's had an ear leaned your way, waiting for you to call. And when you've asked, He's been there for you. Perhaps you really needed help, and He came through for you in an amazing way. Even more than you expected, He helped you or a friend you'd prayed for through a hard time. Or maybe what seemed like a small concern, lifted up to Him, dissipated without trouble.

God starts the relationship with a listening ear—He desires every person to call on Him for salvation. Then He eagerly heeds our confession, adoration, praise, and intercession. But if we won't keep conversation going, by listening to Him, responding in love to His words, and sharing each moment of joy and sorrow with our Creator, we can stall His love. He won't force us to love Him, because that would be manipulation, not love.

But God's listening ear never goes away. We can close the doors of our hearts and stop our lips. Our inattention or unwillingness can ignore His hearing and caring heart. Yet He'll always wait for our voices, because He wants us to reach His heart. He's only a call away. Cry out to Him now.

# IMMEDIATE BLESSINGS

*However, as it is written:*
*"No eye has seen, no ear has heard,*
*no mind has conceived*
*what God has prepared for those who love him."*
1 CORINTHIANS 2:9

God has future blessings in mind for you, but did you realize that this verse is also talking about things you can experience today? Read the context of this passage, and you'll notice that Paul isn't talking about the sweet by-and-by—he's describing his current ministry and the work of the Spirit in the lives of Christians.

So if you've been waiting for heaven to enjoy all the joys and delights of faith, turn around. Look at the blessings you've received today, all the things God has done and is doing in your life, and appreciate them. But don't stop there; you can also start taking advantage of the spiritual mission God has given you. Because God never gives us blessings simply to enjoy—every good thing is meant to be shared.

You don't have to look to another Christian to discover what God has for you. No one in this world can tell you what He has in mind. Verse 10 says God reveals these unseen gifts by His Spirit. So don't hunt through the church, compare your assets to your friends', or even search the world for God's blessings. You won't find them.

Go to the real source—God. He may not share your blessings with the world, but He wants to share them with you. If you ask, He'll show you what He's given and how He wants you to impact others with them.

He has wonderful things in mind for you, so don't wait until eternity—share some of that good news today!

# ADDITIONS AND SUBTRACTIONS

*Do not add to what I command you and do not subtract from it,*
*but keep the commands of the LORD your God that I give you.*
DEUTERONOMY 4:2

My computer grammar check didn't like this verse. It wanted to delete the "not" before "subtract." If I didn't know better, I'd think I had a real person in there, objecting to the meaning of this passage, someone who wanted to change the ~~upcoming~~ Ten Commandments. ~~Perhaps he'd like to get rid of the prohibition against adultery or the command not to have idols.~~ Then he'd be able to do what he wanted and ignore the guilt.

The truth of the matter is, keeping God's Word isn't always easy. Sometimes we'd all like to take out a passage here or there. We'd like to modify some verses to seem less harsh—or less merciful. Or we'd like to add in something we think is better. It's not the things we don't understand in the Bible that bother us as much as the things we *do* understand and don't want to agree with.

But God didn't give us His Word to edit—He gave it as a blessing that will show us how to live. With it we can avoid trouble and receive all the good things God has for us. His commands aren't open to a lot of doubting. They are not unclear, open to differences of opinion, or questionable. ~~These ten quick takes on what it means to believe form the basis for a valuable spiritual life.~~

So instead of editing ~~or rewriting,~~ let's obey. Before long, we won't be questioning, doubting, or disagreeing. Instead we'll be praising God for the work He's done in our lives because we followed His Word just as He commanded.

# GOOD FRIENDS

*Let your foot rarely be in your neighbor's house,*
*Lest he become weary of you and hate you.*
PROVERBS 25:17 NASB

Not only does God want to bless us, He wants us to share that blessing. But in His infinite wisdom, He knows our well-meaning efforts can go awry. It may happen when we first receive Christ and are anxious for our friends to do so, too. We may constantly visit, hoping to show them the joys of God. Or when we move to a new place and don't know many people, we may become dependent on the first people we meet. Eventually our company becomes tiresome, and even the best of friends wants a rest. If someone asks for space, it doesn't mean she doesn't care, but that she needs a rest from our company, so she can give her energies to other life demands. Given space, that friendship may actually grow stronger.

Being a good friend and neighbor doesn't require constant togetherness but does need constant love. Sometimes that means not seeing a friend for awhile, because he's busy at the office. Or she may have a new romance she's spending a lot of time on. Because you don't see your friend every day doesn't mean either of you doesn't care.

Because God cares about us, He gives us tools to build good relationships. This is one of them. If we're wise, we'll heed His Word and make use of this truth to strengthen friendships. Then we'll be in a good position to share our faith with those who don't know Jesus or to encourage our siblings in Christ. And that will be a real blessing.

# WELL-EQUIPPED

*Now the God of peace. . .equip you in every good thing to do His will,*
*working in us that which is pleasing in His sight, through Jesus Christ,*
*to whom be the glory forever and ever. Amen.*
HEBREWS 13:20–21 NASB

God asks us to do many things that don't seem "natural." Hebrews 13:15–19 describes some sacrifices that please God. But we may not easily praise God, feel like doing good, joyfully obey a leader, or pray. We struggle to do right and please Him.

But it is no losing battle. God has assigned us no impossible tasks. True, under our own steam, we cannot fail to sin. But God hasn't made demands of us and deserted us. He works to turn us into the sort of people He wants us to be. Because He equips us to do His will and to please Him, we *can* please Him.

Without God's equipping, we wouldn't understand the Scriptures that describe His desires for us, nor would we experience the heart cleansing of Jesus' blood. We'd try to be good under our own power, experience frustration, and be worse off than before.

Yet because God doesn't want that to be our spiritual end point, He gives us all we need to do good. The power of His Spirit changes our hearts. His Word identifies our path. And Jesus rules our lives.

We don't have to make use of the equipment God offers. Some fail to allow Jesus His rule. But instead of rejoicing in His Son, they live miserable lives, carrying their own broken-down tools that cannot do the job.

How much better to accept God's equipment, for all that do so see His glory firsthand.

# FISHING PRACTICE

*Love suffers long and is kind; love does not envy;*
*love does not parade itself, is not puffed up.*
1 CORINTHIANS 13:4 NKJV

Fly-fishing is really quite easy—if you buy the right equipment, choose the correct flies, practice often, fish in the right places, and learn about the sport. When you see the graceful flick of the fly line as it darts over the fisher's head, pauses briefly, changes direction, then gently lights on the water, a lot of skill and practice has preceded that elegant motion. It's not automatic, requiring physical and mental abilities to combine flawlessly.

Love doesn't come to us automatically, either. When we accept Jesus, He blesses us with His love. But, like fly-fishing, sharing that love contains complexities. We may feel we've nailed down one part of loving well, when we're made aware of somewhere else we've failed. Maybe we've learned to suffer long, but kindness is still difficult—we're like the fisherman who knows how to cast but chooses the wrong fly for his stream.

How do we solve our spiritual dilemma? Maybe we need to consciously practice loving. As we make it a priority to treat other people kindly and with respect, we improve. But just as we won't fly-fish well without the proper stream or lake information, we can't love without help. Unless we know God's Word and follow His Spirit's leading, we'll love clumsily, like a new fisherman who hasn't gotten it all together.

As we draw nearer to God and allow His Spirit access to our lives, the complexities lessen. While we once had to keep an eye on every element, some become more natural. We give thanks for God's work in our lives and begin to tell others of it. Suddenly we're fishing for a different species—people who need to know Jesus.

# SATISFIED!

*You open Your hand*
*And satisfy the desire of every living thing.*
PSALM 145:16 NKJV

Would God give a sparrow all it needs for life and leave a human out of the loop? Obviously the Creator doesn't forget or ignore anything. Without Him, earth wouldn't exist. The universe can't keep its course, apart from His command. But sometimes we wonder if we've somehow disconnected from God. We may seek out all kinds of odd alternatives to God, when our desires seem to have been sidelined and we can't see the way clearly.

All along, God never forgot our needs. The plan hasn't changed, and He hasn't written this verse out of Scripture—even temporarily. He knows all our questions, doubts, and troubles and has an answer for each. But the answers we expect and the ones He gives may be startlingly different. In part, that's because we have different outlooks. We want every desire filled by tomorrow (or at least next year), while He's viewing a longer plan. Our immediate gratification isn't His final goal—but our good is.

Look back on some things you wanted God to do, a week, a year, or several years back. Some may remain unfulfilled, but many have been accomplished. He's seen you through a lot, as you've walked together. And you've been able to testify to His faithfulness as He met those needs. Continue to walk steadily with your Lord, and He'll fulfill many more desires. Then, at the end of life, you'll see that any He left behind were best done so, and you'll offer this one-word testimony: Satisfied!

# SALVATION SATISFACTION

*"With long life I will satisfy him,*
*And show him My salvation."*
PSALM 91:16 NKJV

Would you like an adventuresome life, one in which you saw God do many exciting acts? How would you like to see all the wonderful things He could do, in your life, in the lives of others, and in the world? Getting a front-row seat to God's wonders would be great, wouldn't it?

Well, whether you have a globe-trotting ministry or are a stay-at-home mom, God offers that to you. God plans to prove His salvation to you in many unmistakable ways. He wants to spend many years showing you all the details of His love.

That doesn't mean that every day will be exciting. We all have some dull-as-dust times when we wonder what's going on. But we'll also face enough challenges to assure that life won't be dull. Just when we think we've got a real handle on Christianity, God can show us how little we really know of His personality and character. What had begun to seem quiet and lack challenge quickly becomes a moment-by-moment faith fight.

When we're in those exciting moments, we often wonder if our faith will stand the test. Can we hold on long enough to see the work of God in our lives and the lives of others, or will we give in? Tied up in such worries, we miss the point. God is showing *His* salvation. Dependence on ourselves gets us nowhere, for we cannot be faithful enough. But leaning on God, especially when we feel weakest, brings us safely through the most exciting challenge.

We're not relying on ourselves, but the One who has promised us salvation. What we can't do alone, He's already done for us. Recognize that, and we're satisfied.

# GOOD TASTE!

*O taste and see that the LORD is good:*
*blessed is the man that trusteth in him.*
PSALM 34:8 KJV

God didn't give you food to look at. He provides all you need, but you have to eat it and your body must digest it before that fuel can be of benefit to your body. No one who looks at a steak dinner but bypasses it gains the energy food gives for hard work. A salad won't do you much good if it never gets past your lips.

It's the same way with experiencing God. You could walk down an aisle, say the words of commitment, and never go further. Lots of folks have done just that. But none of them can claim to have tasted God. They haven't seen the best of the Savior, and if they tried to give a testimony, they wouldn't have much to say.

But faithful believers walk with God, watch the way He works, and appreciate the impact salvation has on all who act on His promises. Though the faithful ones often struggle, not one of them fails, for God brings blessings in the midst of every hardship. Experiencing His love in their own lives and the lives of others, strong Christians taste God's goodness and increase their own trust in the Savior.

God doesn't limit any Christian's ability to taste His goodness. Nor is He stingy with His blessings. This open invitation to experience and trust can be accepted by all who believe. So what's keeping us from taking Him at His word and experiencing the blessing in our own lives? Nothing but our own questions and fears. So let's spit out all doubt today and take a good taste of God.

# REALLY FREE?

*"Therefore if the Son makes you free, you shall be free indeed."*
JOHN 8:36 NKJV

Most people in the Greater New York Area agree: Though driving can be challenging here, we don't command the worst drivers. We usually cede that honor to Boston, where streets are narrower and frequently one-way. But we might be the most discourteous drivers. People frequently act as if they are the only ones on the road!

Most discourteous drivers have been given the freedom to slip behind the wheel, place the key in the ignition, start up, and head for the road. They have a driver's license to prove it. And many see it just that way—they have a license to do just as they please.

Caught up in their own independence, these folks have missed out on the truth that they aren't really free at all: They can't seem to do good. Allow cars in ahead of you during a traffic jam, and the drivers you're being gracious to hesitate. Are you really going to let them go, or are you plotting to cut them off at the last minute? People become so used to bad behavior, they can't believe in any good.

Unbelievers are like that in other areas of life, too. They can't believe in a good God because Satan's chains bind them so tight. Rejecting God seems only sensible, based on their life experience.

They'll never know otherwise, unless they see someone who is free indeed—who lets them in on the highway or returns good for evil in other ways. So think of your daily Christian testimony as liberating—who knows what simple act could help another understand your freedom to do right, not just to do what you want.

# GOOD THINGS

*I know that nothing is better for them than to rejoice,*
*and to do good in their lives, and also that every man should eat*
*and drink and enjoy the good of all his labor—it is the gift of God.*
ECCLESIASTES 3:12–13 NKJV

When God gives you a good thing—a new house, a child, or a special job—do you hesitate to enjoy it? Do you fear paying a price because it's just "too good"? Or do you feel guilty because you have something another person doesn't have?

Where does the idea that Christians should not enjoy life come from? Not from the Bible. Perhaps it's a lie straight from hell, because Scripture often speaks of the blessings God gives His people—and some are physical.

That doesn't mean enjoyment is our primary goal in life. We shouldn't mainly seek out wealth and fortune. God describes these things as fleeting, and putting our trust in them will only lead to sorrow. An " 'eat, drink, and be merry' " lifestyle (Luke 12:19) isn't appropriate for the Christian; Jesus' parable clearly shows that. When our priorities become messed up and we put things and pleasure before God, we can expect trouble.

But that doesn't mean we can't rejoice when God gives us worldly goods and can't make wise use of them. When we thank God for His blessings and use them properly—to help others and support our families in a responsible Christian lifestyle—those temporary things become blessings He can use through us. That's just what God intended.

If you work hard for your money and are rewarded, you can appreciate God's gift and use it for blessing. Then you'll have done right and won't be the only one who rejoices.

# FULLY BLESSED

*"And there you shall eat before the LORD your God,*
*and you shall rejoice in all to which you have put your hand,*
*you and your households, in which the LORD your God has blessed you."*
DEUTERONOMY 12:7 NKJV

When the Israelites were ready to head into the Promised Land, God had Moses remind them of their past and His faithfulness to them. The prophet warned them not to fall into idolatry and told them God was going to give them a new place to worship. This promise follows those instructions.

God wasn't trying to make their new life hard on His people or deny them good things. Instead He planned on bringing them much joy—both through the physical blessings of good land and a fulfilled spiritual promise. Those warnings were meant to bring them only the best He had to offer.

We, too, have seen God turn us aside from places we want to go or things we want to do. Maybe He's denied us a desired job, the "perfect" mate, or some other good thing. When that's happened, maybe it's because it wouldn't be as wonderful as we think. What we see through rose-colored glasses, God observes clearly. And because all He wants is our good, He stops us before we get involved.

But when we put aside the things that would distract us from Him and work or worship where He wants us to, our lives are fully blessed. We can worship Him for the things He has given us—the physical and spiritual joys that leap off our tongues as we think of all our Savior has given.

# EMPTY OR FILLED?

*"Blessed are those who hunger and thirst for righteousness,*
*For they shall be filled."*
MATTHEW 5:6 NKJV

Spiritual emptiness doesn't seem like much of a blessing, does it? It's something we usually try to avoid, instead of welcoming it to our lives. So why would God call us blessed when we feel this way?

Maybe it's because feeling isn't all there is to faith. Hunger and thirst pain us, but they can lead us to deeper faith, if we allow them to. Though a bad experience doesn't feel good at first, in the end, it can become a blessing. It's not the hurt that's good, but the things it can bring into our lives, if we see it through to the end.

Hunger and thirst are signs of emptiness, but they also indicate a desire for God. While the hollowness that shows us our need for Him isn't fun, it's actually a good spiritual sign—it shows we're on track in our spiritual growth. Only a person who wants to know more of God, go more deeply into His love, will hunger and thirst for Him. Those without this hunger often are not satisfied, but self-satisfied. Because they cannot feel their need for Him, they cannot grow and become filled with His Spirit in new ways.

My dad used to describe some things as being "full of emptiness." A Christian can be that way, but not forever. That emptiness doesn't last long, as the faithful one turns to Him and asks to be filled by His Spirit or with His love. It may not happen in an instant, but before long, that emptiness disappears in a new spiritual challenge or a rejoicing hope. What once was empty *has* been filled.

# BEST OF BOTH WORLDS

*"For God so loved the world that he gave his only Son,*
*so that everyone who believes in him will not perish*
*but have eternal life."*
JOHN 3:16 NLT

You've known someone who looked for love in the worst places. Desperate to feel wanted, that man or woman jumped from love interest to love interest, but the results were rarely good.

But all of us, if we were honest, could admit we desperately need love. This harsh world attacks us if we have no one to love and be loved by. Our empty hearts begin to despair when love seems to pass us by.

What many hurting people—even some Christians—fail to recognize is that human love only goes so far. Exciting romance feels good, but it doesn't solve every problem; in fact, it can be the beginning of even bigger troubles, if you're not careful. Then the hurt of love gone wrong can dry out your soul. It's not the love this world is founded on, so it can never give us all we need.

But there's one love that every person, weak or strong, can enjoy. It won't lead to a bad place or break a heart. It doesn't die out, as so many romances do, and no one feels used at the end of it. God's love is perfect, so no baggage ties it down or ruins it. Not only that, God's love never ends. He plans to bring us into eternity with Him. So the love that buoys us up today never disappears.

But link romantic love and the love of the Savior, and you have a winning combination. It's the best of both worlds!

# TONGUE AND HEART

*But whoever keeps His word,*
*in him the love of God has truly been perfected.*
*By this we know that we are in Him:*
*the one who says he abides in Him ought himself*
*to walk in the same manner as He walked.*

1 JOHN 2:5–6 NASB

Want to fully experience God's perfect love? Then obey Him. Talking a good line about being a faithful Christian might seem nice, but it doesn't quite cut it. God knows His really devoted servants, and He doesn't recognize them by their mouths, but their hearts and their actions.

That doesn't mean our mouths aren't part of our obedience. The words we say are one piece of our testimony: When we speak kind words instead of harsh critiques, when we avoid saying anything that would bring God into disgrace, we use our mouths to do His will. But when we speak to bring ourselves honor, instead of God, we've clearly missed the boat.

Those about us won't miss the truth, though. Non-Christians recognize those who mean what they say and live it out, too. These believers frequently get respect for their commitment, even from others who don't agree with them. But the Christian who talks a lot about his commitment but can't stop to help a person in trouble or hesitates to help a coworker who's part of her team clearly identifies a critical faith weakness.

When we walk the way Jesus did, like Him, we obey the Father. Instead of taking the glory for ourselves, we lift up the One who really deserves it. That's when that perfect love not only comes from our tongues, but from our hearts, too.

# UNENDING HOPE

*But may the God of all grace,*
*who called us to His eternal glory by Christ Jesus,*
*after you have suffered awhile, perfect, establish,*
*strengthen, and settle you.*
1 PETER 5:10 NKJV

When we suffer, hope still springs up in us. That's true for all people, but as Christians we are especially able to continue anticipating the best, even when life tries to make us doubt it. Why? Because we don't base our hope on this earth or a Pollyanna attitude that ignores wrongdoing or disaster. Our hope's firmly set in the God of all grace, who has already showered us with blessings. His faithfulness, throughout our Christian walk, has proved Him, and we know He will not desert us. Even the worst this earth does cannot have the final word in our lives. It may work to improve and strengthen us, but it cannot break us if we cling to Jesus.

Sometimes, in the midst of trials, we receive the best blessings. When we show our loved ones how much we care by standing firm, through financial trials or challenges to our love, we more fully appreciate and deepen those relationships. If we stand by our churches when they are under strain, we may build a stronger faith ourselves, while developing a spiritually awesome community.

Whatever our situation and no matter what pain we suffer, we must recognize that suffering is never the end point. Most suffering lasts only a time on earth, but none of it is permanent. Even death, when it comes, is not final for believers. Eternity awaits us, where we will be perfect, established, strengthened, and settled forever.

# ALL ETERNITY

*He has made everything beautiful in its time.*
*Also He has put eternity in their hearts,*
*except that no one can find out the work*
*that God does from beginning to end.*
ECCLESIASTES 3:11 NKJV

Have you looked at God's stars and marveled as they lit the velvet-dark sky? Watched a sunset in which the sky is tinted from the lightest blue on the horizon to a deep tone above and delighted in God's paintbrush? Then you've seen Him make things beautiful in their time. A few hours later, those delights disappeared into the daylight, which has its own set of glories.

Though we appreciate our changing world, we only understand so much of it. Even the best scientists cannot describe every detail of our world, from its first day to the present. And if they could, they still couldn't so combine it with beauty that we could appreciate both simultaneously. God is so much greater than we can be. None of us can fully aspire to His greatness.

Though we're not up to the task of fully understanding all He does, this glorious God still wants us near Him. We can't meet Him on His own terms, yet He wants us so much that He offered us the great blessing of eternity in our hearts. Even the beauty of a magnificent world can't fill our hearts and souls. He has given us the desire to spend all eternity with Him.

So while you're gazing at that beautiful sky, don't forget to praise the One who created it and you—and be thankful that you were one He decided to share eternity with.

# THE SPACIOUS PLACE

*"He brought me out into a spacious place;*
*he rescued me because he delighted in me."*
2 SAMUEL 22:20

Have you ever wondered why God chose to save you and not your brother, sister, neighbor, or friend? Perhaps you've looked at yourself honestly and decided, if it were your choice, you might have saved another person and left yourself behind. (But how glad you feel that God decided to pour His grace out on you!) Then you start to wonder if He'll ever give the same blessing to that non-Christian.

You could wonder about these questions for a lifetime and still never have an answer. God doesn't give us the whys of His salvation. He's not obliged to tell us His reasons for doing anything, much less saving us. Nor does He have to tell us if He plans on saving another.

It's enough for us to know that God did save us, and He did it to please Himself. But that doesn't really end the matter. David's psalm, of which this is only a part, also talks about the believer's responsibility to obey God. Will that loved one hear the Good News? Perhaps only if you bear it. And if the message isn't heard, there is still prayer. Few of us hear the message once and run to God. But hard hearts can still be opened with consistent prayer.

Living in the spacious place doesn't mean we want to stay there alone. We'd rather share our space with those emotionally close to us. But if they won't come, perhaps another will. As we share His news, others join us in that spacious place that never becomes crowded—there's always more room in God's love. He's always delighted to share it with another of His children.

# UNDER CONTROL

*He covers the heavens with clouds, provides rain for the earth,*
*and makes the green grass grow in mountain pastures.*
PSALM 147:8 NLT

We may complain when rain washes out the church picnic, but in the middle of a drought, our view changes entirely. We search the sky for clouds as our lawns or crops wither and die. As reservoir levels dip, we may even begin to pray seriously for a change of weather. When rain comes—not just drizzle, but a downpour—we feel God's blessing.

How often do we see bad weather as a blessing? We're more likely to lament the game that got canceled or the snow that made our holiday visit impossible.

Let's remember that the weather is not ours to command, but God's. Unlike our daily schedules, we cannot control how much rain we get in a year or when the next storm will come. If that were left up to us, we'd probably quickly discover we're happy to leave the details to the Almighty. Keeping up with weather all over the world for even a single day would tax us beyond our powers.

Instead, we need to give thanks even for the daily blessings God offers us—rain that keeps wells and reservoirs filled, enough snow to make a white Christmas but not impede traffic, or sunshine for a special outing.

When the weather doesn't go "our way," we can still thank God that He's in control. Maybe our date wasn't more important than a growing harvest or a well filled to near capacity. And when we have an overabundance of rain or snow, we can count on it that He knows what He's doing. After all, He has it all under control, doesn't He?

# HELP FOR UNBELIEF

*Immediately the father of the child cried out and said with tears,*
*"Lord, I believe; help my unbelief!"*

MARK 9:24 NKJV

Since my days as a young Christian, I've treasured this verse, perhaps because I relate so definitively to the man who spoke those words. In a crisis of situation and faith, when his child was in danger and he struggled to believe, he discovered his weakness. Agonizing at the fate of his son and his own inability even to do what Jesus reminds him he needs to do—have faith—he asks the Master to help his unbelief.

No doubt the man already knew faith was the solution, but, like us, found it hard to put that knowledge into action. To Jesus, he admitted his imperfect faith, and in that moment, the blessing of God unexpectedly fell on him. But it shouldn't have been such a surprise, really. After all, that's the main message God has to get through to us: We can't do anything alone—even have faith. All belief comes as a gift from Him. But neither will God give us the ability to believe and then cast us out on our own. That would be like the frustrating god the Deists believed in, who supposedly created the world, then left it to itself, to work out its own solutions to problems.

Jesus didn't give us faith to impart frustration. He offered it to us so we can cling to Him, obey the Father, and spend an eternity in praise. So a feeling of frustration may indicate we're attempting to go it alone instead of giving up our doubts and questions to the Lord who promised to help us. A simple "Help!" to Jesus is all it takes to turn that situation around.

# THE WORLD OR JESUS?

*For if you wander beyond the teaching of Christ,*
*you will not have fellowship with God.*
*But if you continue in the teaching of Christ,*
*you will have fellowship with both the Father and the Son.*
2 JOHN 9 NLT

Plenty of non-Christians denigrate Christians for their "narrow-mindedness." They prefer to believe their own ideas are creative, open-minded, or freer than the teachings of Jesus. Before long, they may even have Christians wondering if their beliefs—or lack of them—are better than the "restrictive" teachings of our Lord.

Before you follow those ideas or feel as if you're hopelessly out-dated, reread this passage from John's second letter. John probably received similar complaints from the Gnostics, whom you might call the New Agers of his day. The fledgling church, standing up to wrong teachings, had a hard time of it. People didn't approve of Christianity any more then than they do now. Christians faced much opposition, and John had to remind believers just what they'd put their faith in.

Any Christian in any age can wander off into teaching that has little or nothing to do with Jesus. But will it really be better, as the non-Christian claims? John reminds Christians of the consequence of that kind of change: losing touch with Jesus. Those of us who have come to believe in Him treasure our contact with the Savior. That's why Christians spend so much time in prayer and Bible study. Would we really want to give up the intimate relationship with Him for any-thing a human has to offer?

The choice is simple: the world or Jesus? Will we wander to something better? No! We can't give up anything that's better than He is.

# THE BITTER END

*"Don't call me Naomi," she told them.*
*"Instead, call me Mara,*
*for the Almighty has made life very bitter for me."*
RUTH 1:20 NLT

Naomi's making a pun here that gets a little lost in the translation, unless you read your Bible notes. Her name means "pleasant," but since life hadn't been very good for her for a long time, she asks her people to call her Mara, or "bitter" instead.

Naomi and her family moved out of Israel, when a famine threatened, and went to Moab. After more than ten years, her husband and sons died. Naomi returned to Bethlehem with nothing but one of her daughters-in-law, Ruth. It wasn't a happy return, so when people asked, "Is this really Naomi?" she responded with the above sentences.

Like Naomi, we may have bitter days. Everything that surrounds our lives seems unpalatable. Perhaps we see no hope for the future and could respond as she did. But like Naomi, when we feel that way, we are not looking at the end of the story. As long as we live, God is not finished writing our tale. This bitter patch may be the dark part of the story that just precedes the happiest parts of our lives. If we give up, we'll never reach the best part of the story.

When we hold on 'til the bitter end, like Naomi, we may find it isn't bitter at all. She found herself the center of a loving family, with a grandson to carry on the family name. Best of all, God used that infant to create something of eternal value—he became a forebear of God's Son, Jesus. Could anything that created the Light of the World remain bitter for long?

# DELIGHTFUL DAY

*He also brought me out into a broad place;*
*He delivered me because He delighted in me.*
PSALM 18:19 NKJV

Following a blizzard touted as "the storm of the century," my bassets decided to do "snow angels" in the more than fourteen-inch snowbank called my front yard. Though their backs were just about even with the top of it, they bounced atop the white stuff and ploughed on, leaving leg and belly marks.

I admit I laughed, though I also kept an eye on them to be sure they were safe. It was really rather fun to see them enjoying themselves and taking on a new challenge. They'd never seen this much snow.

Somewhat like a pet owner who gets a lot of enjoyment from the animal's antics, I imagine God delights in watching us take on new things, enjoy the world He's created for us, and learn more of Him. He didn't create us to become our taskmaster, but because He wanted to share things with us: not only in eternity, but here on earth, too. Though Scripture contains many serious warnings and guidelines, there are frequent indications of the joy He has in His creation, and part of that creation is us.

So while we're trying to do the right thing and follow His way intently, let's not forget that we can also simply rejoice in the God who saved us. He delivered us because He delighted in us, and He wants us to delight in Him, too.

Make this a truly delightful day as you worship the Savior who loves you in so many ways. Remember, He wants to share the fun with you, too.

# REDIRECTION

*For whom the LORD loves He corrects,*
*Just as a father the son in whom he delights.*
PROVERBS 3:12 NKJV

In today's "independent" society, the idea of correcting your child isn't popular. So much so that a parent with a disruptive child often hesitates to do anything in public beyond a weak "Johnny, stop that." To do more might court criticism or even the risk of losing the child altogether.

But God denies the current child-raising theory that hesitates to redirect a child with firmness. He says a loving parent will correct the child properly—with love and kindness, but with enough firmness to make it stick. Not to do that would be to ignore the child's best interests.

We've experienced that kind of correction in our own spiritual lives; and though we may have doubted it was a blessing when we first felt it, as we've grown in Christ, we've learned how right this verse is. God bothers to tell us when we've done wrong or missed His path because He cares where we end up. Though we initially find the correction distasteful, in the end we learn it's done not because God is stern but because He wants us to experience the best life possible. We can only know we've done wrong when He helps us see the better way we should have gone.

The kind of independence that ignores God's correction costs us heavily. We've seen it in those who reject Him entirely or who claim to accept Christ but never walk in His way. Do we really want to live that way, or will we take the course correction our Savior has to offer?

# HONEY TO THE SOUL

*Kind words are like honey—sweet to the soul*
*and healthy for the body.*
PROVERBS 16:24 NLT

One of the great blessings of the Christian life is a kind word, spoken just when you need to hear it.

Look at the unbelieving world, and how often will you find kindness? Once in awhile, in a rare human being. More often, you'll experience criticism and condemnation.

One thing that should set Christians apart from unbelievers is a caring kindness. When you don't find kindness in the church, something has gone wrong. A critical spirit isn't from God and can't help the soul and body.

But we also can't expect the church always to agree with all we do. When we've fallen into wrongdoing, it is the responsibility of caring Christians to confront us lovingly and set us on the right track. When we respond to that correction, we can again feel the kindness of those who have loved us well enough to tell us we've been wrong. We might have missed it when we were doing wrong, but wise Christians will still have used it to draw us back to the right path.

People have a hard time hearing critics, unless they know care is also there. A combination of correction and kindness often makes the difference in whether or not those words are really heard. Honey spreads easily on the soul, while criticism feels like sand in an open wound.

Whether you need to encourage or redirect another Christian, are you speaking kind words? If so, their sweetness may bring just the healing God has in mind.

# SWEET WORDS

*How sweet are your words to my taste;*
*they are sweeter than honey.*
PSALM 119:103 NLT

When you're looking for some sweetness in a sour life, turn to Scripture. Read the story of Joseph, who triumphed over his brothers' jealousy and slavery. Discover how brave Esther saved her people. Follow the soul-saving story of Jesus' ministry. Or read the Psalms, for encouragement from a king.

As you read, feel blessed. Non-Christians don't get this feeling about Scripture. To them, without the Holy Spirit's prompting, the Bible remains a closed book. Some read it but come away with erroneous ideas about it. Others never seem to get beyond a few pages.

But the Scriptures are God's huge love letter to His own people. As even the newest believer reads attentively, His mercy becomes clear. Yet a lifelong believer can read the same passage and see something new again and again. God's relationship with the Christian constantly grows, through His Book, and with it He shows new depth at every stage of growth.

Don't get caught up in the mysteries of Scripture and miss the plain, blessed truth of how much Jesus loves you today. Over and over, in many ways, He's made it clear that He cared enough to die for you. Rather than enjoying heaven with only the angels, it was important to Him to share it with humans, too. All He asks is that you believe in His Son.

He's left you the story of Jesus in His Book, but that's not all He offers. He wants His Spirit to help you understand and make those words sweet. Have you read those words and felt the sweetness of His heart?

# TEACHING APPRECIATION

*We reject all shameful and underhanded methods.*
*We do not try to trick anyone, and we do not distort the word of God.*
*We tell the truth before God, and all who are honest know that.*

2 CORINTHIANS 4:2 NLT

Has a faithful Bible teacher opened the Word to you? Did you appreciate the blessing that person has been to you? Maybe you said a word or two to let the teacher know how thankful you were. Or you passed the truth you'd learned to another, to share the message. Teachers always appreciate it when their lessons are carried to other people, who also grow through that knowledge.

But not every teacher receives appreciation—many good, solid Christians face trouble, through no fault of their own. Paul, who provided a testimony designed to bring the gospel to the Western world, didn't have it easy when it came to the Corinthian church. Accusers told lies about him and his agenda. These false teachers tried to make the apostle look bad so they could mislead the people and gain some authority. Paul frequently redirected the Corinthians to the truth.

Despite the lies and gossip, Paul didn't give up on the Corinthians. Faithful to God, the apostle recognized the need to stand firm. Though it must have hurt him deeply, he didn't let their negative response cloud God's message or purpose for his life.

Whether you've been taught by a steadfast friend or a "professional Christian," a pastor or professor, if you've been blessed, don't stab that person in the back. Avoid leaving without appreciating the impact of that teaching on your thoughts and deeds. Support the person who brought you God's faithful message—and somehow, pass it on to another who needs a blessing today.

# ONE GREAT DAY

*Every tongue will confess that Jesus Christ is Lord,*
*to the glory of God the Father.*
PHILIPPIANS 2:11 NLT

Someday, Jesus' greatness will be unavoidable. Even the greatest doubters and those who lived in a fashion entirely contradictory to His teachings will have to admit He rules heaven and earth. It will be a hard day for unbelievers. Imagine their having to admit very publicly that they've been so wrong. Not only will they have to accept their huge mistake, but they must bow down to the Jesus whom they so misjudged. Their stiff knees will finally bend before the Lord of heaven and earth (Philippians 2:10).

But on that great day, what joy faithful followers will feel. In one moment, all the truths we've put faith in will become concrete before us. Instead of simply trusting, we'll have perfect proof that our faith was right. Before our eyes will be all the things we have understood spiritually for so very long.

Where the doubters feel agony, we will experience the purest pleasure. Giving Jesus the glory on that day will be our greatest delight—one we look forward to with anticipation even now.

We yearn for that glorious day, but until it comes, the work Jesus gave us is not yet done. Faith, lived out consistently, may turn some doubting hearts to the Savior. Then instead of being horrified by their wrong judgment, they, too, will share the blessing of praise for Jesus.

We who once deserved condemnation have seen it turned aside for mercy—fulfilling the message our Savior had all along. Let's share that with as many as we can.

# RUBBISH PILE

*More than that, I count all things to be loss in view*
*of the surpassing value of knowing Christ Jesus my Lord,*
*for whom I have suffered the loss of all things,*
*and count them but rubbish so that I may gain Christ.*

PHILIPPIANS 3:8 NASB

Have you ever feared giving something to Jesus? Perhaps you worry if you were more faithful He'd ask you to leave your job and become a missionary. Or you'd have to change your career to something less worldly. Satan is good at putting such thoughts in our heads at the very moment God challenges us to greater commitment. Often, that simple fear works, and we back down on our faith.

Paul didn't back down. Called to live for Jesus on the road to Damascus, he answered the call, though it meant separating from his "career" as a religious Jew. For a time, neither Jews nor the followers of Jesus accepted him, because he'd switched so suddenly from persecuting the Christians to being one of them. The new Christian was out in the cold for awhile, until both sides knew what to believe about him.

But Paul testifies that his life-changing decision was the right one. It made him lose every valuable worldly possession, but it gave him the one thing that was worth having: Jesus. He knew that if he had to make the choice again, he'd do it just the same.

Is there something you need to place on the rubbish pile to follow Jesus? Be certain that no matter what you leave there, it will be so insignificant, compared to the joy of a closer walk with Him.

# WORD ACCOUNT

*"A good person produces good deeds from a good heart,*
*and an evil person produces evil deeds from an evil heart.*
*Whatever is in your heart determines what you say."*
LUKE 6:45 NLT

Is a man good or evil? Look at his spiritual fruit, and you'll know. Has he used his gifts for God's good, or his own? Is a woman really as holy as she claims? Don't listen to her words, but look at the ministry she heads. Does it accomplish goals that glorify God? Do her business practices follow God's Word?

Works don't save a Christian, but they show a lot about that believer's walk. They may not always indicate whether or not she decided to make a commitment to Jesus, but they will surely show how she lived it out. And if, throughout life, he never does a thing for God, perhaps the words he spoke didn't quite reach his heart.

One particularly powerful way people show their commitment is by their words. Though anyone can tell a few convincing lies, over time the truth of those words becomes clear. Inconsistencies start to show up, and eventually others catch on if the so-called believer wanted to buy eternal fire insurance, instead of follow Jesus. What's in the heart comes out, one way or another.

That's why consistency is so important for any Christian. Non-believers aren't fooled when we say one thing and do another or do things even they know don't glorify God. They can tell the faithful Christians from those who only want the name.

Your words give an account for whatever's going on inside you. Are they telling the world you're evil or good?

# FAITHFUL TESTIMONY

*Now Stephen, a man full of God's grace and power,*
*did great wonders and miraculous signs among the people.*
*Opposition arose, however.*
ACTS 6:8–9

It's not uncommon, when you're doing a work for God's kingdom, to face opposition. Just when a ministry is beginning to bear fruit or when you're helping others greatly, little things may cause disruptions or larger issues may bring it to a halt.

Instead of giving yourself over to the frustration, recognize that even very prominent Christians have suffered similar problems. It's not uncommon for nonbelievers to become jealous of a good work. Like Stephen, you may have run aground on someone else's attitudes. But whatever the problem, if you've been faithful, you are on the right track and God will stand firm with you.

The new deacon's problems didn't come from his own weakness or lack of faith. Scripture makes it clear Stephen gave a powerful witness to God's work. His testimony to the Sanhedrin was a model sermon— it just wasn't popular with people who didn't want to hear the truth.

When troubles come against us, as they did against Stephen, we can follow his example and continue to bear God's witness. Because the deacon opened his mouth, despite the danger, God gave him a potent testimony. Even as his opponents stoned him, Stephen spoke of the power of faith in Jesus.

Chances might be slim we would lose our lives for our faith, but we may fear loss of work, family, or popularity. The God who remained faithful to Stephen also supports us. If we stand firm, no matter what the outcome, like that first-century deacon, we will effectively lift up His name.

# FULLY JOYOUS

*"I have told you this so that you will be filled with my joy.*
*Yes, your cup of joy will overflow!"*
JOHN 15:11 TLB

Overflowing joy! We tend to connect that with a feeling of freedom. When a wonderful, unusual event occurs or when we are released from a burden of fear, this is the way we respond.

Do we also associate joy with obedience to God? Maybe not as often. Yet the "this" Jesus talked about in the above verse was the obedience that caused the disciples to remain in His love. You can't separate Christian love, obedience, and joy. They work together to describe God's kingdom to us.

As long as we set our ideas above God's and don't take His commands seriously enough to obey them, we won't feel the intense joy of knowing Him deeply. Separation occurs, because we will not submit to Him. We've tacitly said we don't believe God knows what He's talking about in His Word. And He takes that very personally.

As long as we intentionally disobey God, we cannot experience full joy. But those who seek to do His will, though they don't achieve it perfectly, experience an increasingly profound relationship with Him. God knows our weaknesses and does not require perfection before He communes with us. But He desires that we commit ourselves to Him and follow His Word. When we consistently walk with Him, He connects with us and aids us in living out His Word. The more we live for Him, the more our joy communicates itself to the world, just as God ordained.

Finally, in heaven, we'll become completely joyous, as we meet with the God we have trusted so long. As our delight in our Redeemer pours from us, we'll sing His praises eternally.

# FRUIT CHECK

*"By this My Father is glorified, that you bear much fruit;*
*so you will be My disciples."*
JOHN 15:8 NKJV

God didn't design us to be couch potatoes—He wants us to be fruit bearers instead. Jesus gives us a picture of a grapevine, laden with fruit.

Can any of us ever bear too much fruit? Probably not. But we *can* put our efforts into bearing the wrong kind of fruit—getting caught up in the small, useless things makes our fruit tiny and sour, instead of the refreshing sustenance it's supposed to be.

We do that when we "play church" but forget what the church is really about. Perhaps we started out with good intentions but got bogged down by methods to reach out to others. Or maybe the way we organize our church became more important than what we believe.

Jesus didn't invite us into His kingdom to organize ourselves into eternity. He wanted us to share real life that weighs down the vine, it's so heavy with benefits. But we often replace that with a rule-keeping legalism that redefines and neutralizes the seemingly faithful church.

The difference between the fruit bearer and the rule keeper is a strong connection to God. Those firmly tapped into Him through His Son, Jesus, can feed the hungry. Anyone caught up in rules doesn't have much to bite into.

All Christians want to be heavily fruit bearing. But we can't be that if we have a weak Jesus connection. A Christian who doesn't spend much time with the Savior bears little fruit. But a believer who taps into Him every day, spending time talking and listening to Him, through prayer and the Word, begins to burgeon with it. Opportunities to reach out will come, and the fruit becomes heavier all the time.

# LIGHTENED BURDENS

*"Come to Me, all you who labor and are heavy laden,
and I will give you rest."*
MATTHEW 11:28 NKJV

After a long, frustrating day at work, we all know what it is to crave rest. Whether we use our muscles or brains on the job, we know what it is to be worn out.

But people wear out spiritually, too. When we don't make it to church for a couple of weeks, even if we had imperative reasons why we couldn't make it, the wear and tear on our spirits can begin to show. Or perhaps we've been faithful in a ministry, but it hasn't left us much time to relax, and our bodies are beginning to tell us we've overdone it.

We need to use some sense when we're tired. Maybe what we really need is help so we can make it to church—a ride from a friend or help with whatever keeps us away—or a little extra rest. But we shouldn't stop at the sensible things, because we could rest all week and still feel heavily burdened. Extra sleep or relaxation can only do so much, though they're a good place to start.

Jesus also tells us to come to Him when weariness floods our souls. We can do that many ways. More time than usual in prayer and personal Bible study may help. Or perhaps we can benefit from listening to a special Christian speaker or reading an encouraging book. Whatever we need for refreshment and wherever we turn, our focus needs to be on God. When we drink deeply at His well, the energy will begin to flow.

Then our burdens will become light, and we'll be ready for work again.

# FIVE-YEAR PLAN

*A man's steps are of the LORD;*
*How then can a man understand his own way?*
PROVERBS 20:24 NKJV

Some people like to engage in five-year planning. They set a course, deciding where they'd like their career and personal life to be in a few years. That way they can decide how to handle their lives.

Planning isn't a bad thing—such an exercise may help us organize our lives and establish some goals. But we need to recognize that our plan won't be the final word. There's too much change in the world. If we expect to reach a certain job position but experience a layoff, our plan may be disrupted. Or we may want to marry in a few years but not meet anyone we care to share our lives with. After marriage perhaps we expect to have children, but the babies never come—or come more quickly than expected.

When we consider ways to handle life, whether we try to look ahead five years or one, it's best to recognize that God controls our days. Planning with that in mind will be more successful than a schedule made up simply of our own desires.

If we allow God to lead us in the path He has planned, we won't understand every challenge or disappointment we face. We may not clearly envision our position two years from now, but we will know we're headed in the right way. When we follow Him, nothing that happens stymies the Creator. No plan fails because we're confused. So let's trust our days, weeks, months, and years to Him. If we give ourselves completely to the best planner this world has to offer, we can never end up in a ditch—and all we do will lead to eternal blessings.

# IN THE SHEPHERD'S ARMS

*He will feed His flock like a shepherd;*
*He will gather the lambs with His arm,*
*And carry them in His bosom,*
*And gently lead those who are with young.*
ISAIAH 40:11 NKJV

We may not appreciate being compared to sheep. We like to think of ourselves as sophisticated, admirable individuals, not such silly, often-dirty animals. But God's comparison isn't really unfair: We, like sheep, foolishly allow distractions to draw us from His care. No matter how we try, daily sin begrimes us.

Despite our messy state, when we call out in need, our Savior lifts us up and carries us in His arms or gently directs us when we're at our weakest. His soft heart cares for us, even when we aren't especially sophisticated or admirable. As Jesus' arms wrap around us, His warm compassion floods our souls. When His children feel pain, God's comfort is so profoundly tender that nothing equals it. No one heals hearts like Jesus. Human empathy can't reach the places His Spirit entwines and soothes.

The same powerful God who rules the universe, corrects His erring children, and judges the wicked is also intensely kind to those He loves. Though wrongdoers rightly fear Him, His children need never doubt His gracious heart. He has given us a place in His love, and nothing can separate us from it.

No matter how smelly and foolish we've become, when we call on Jesus, just as the sheep bleats out its need for the shepherd, He gathers us up, dirt and all. Cuddled in His arms, no harm comes to us. If He leads us down a path, we need not fear attack.

All that matters is that we're with Him again and never want to be apart.

# HEAVENLY REWARD

*The world and its desires pass away,*
*but the man who does the will of God lives forever.*
1 JOHN 2:17

Have you enjoyed a special meal? Delighted in our beautiful daylight world or the stars that canopy our nights? God gave us those things to enjoy, but they are gone in a flash. Knowing they disappear quickly, we don't try to hold on to them. Who would think of making more of short-term blessings than we should?

But Christians still get caught up in many worldly blessings that last little longer than those quick ones. We may be tempted to worship money or the things it buys, status, or passionate romance. So the apostle warns us not to put a lot of stock in them. Just like a beautiful sunrise or celebration meal, they will be here today and gone tomorrow.

Why does God give us such ephemeral things? Nothing good enters our hands that we cannot use to glorify Him. Whether we use that meal to reconnect with a loved one or we praise Him for the beauties of nature He gives, we have properly handled His blessings. It's the same with everything else, from money to romance. Those we employ to glorify God gain eternal value. Anything we use for our own gain goes the way of a midnight sky.

If we could haul a chest full of cash to heaven, what use would it be? There, no one needs more than God's eternal provision. Those who express their love for Him on earth, by spending their blessings wisely, ready themselves for an impressive heavenly reward—one that surely impresses the only One who needs to be pleased.

# HEAVENLY BARGAIN

*"But lay up for yourselves treasures in heaven,*
*where neither moth nor rust destroys*
*and where thieves do not break in and steal."*
MATTHEW 6:20 NKJV

I magine, you can start a heavenly treasure chest while you're still here on earth! But you can't fill it with dollars, pounds, or pesos. Though no earthly currency transports to heaven, even the poorest person on earth can lay aside eternal blessings.

That's because heavenly treasures have nothing to do with our legal tender—no government creates or backs it. God's riches can't be exchanged on paper or metal. They're collected in a currency of the heart that consists of things like forgiveness, humility, and charitable deeds.

Forgive a neighbor who did you wrong, and you're the one who pays the price, yet you do not lose whatever you gave. God stores it up in His eternal memory, and when you reach heaven, you'll find an even greater value placed upon your response than could have been given on earth. Not only that, the benefit doesn't last only for as long as your neighbor lives next to you, but forever!

On top of that, any good thing you do because you love Jesus won't disappear. Thieves can't remove it from you, the government can't tax you on it, and fire won't burn it down. Nothing can destroy it or take the shine from it.

When you think about it, even if you have plenty of cash, do you want to use it to buy a few extra clothes or support God's kingdom? Are you putting your money into moth food or feeding a person's soul? One lasts a few years and the other for eternity. Which is the better bargain?

# RESCUE COMING

*The righteous face many troubles,*
*but the LORD rescues them from each and every one.*
PSALM 34:19 NLT

Wouldn't you like to be rescued from every problem in life? It would be nice never to have to deal with any difficulties, wouldn't it?

Well, bad news, the Bible isn't promising you'll live in some imaginary paradise, where trouble never crosses your path. But the good news is that though you face many troubles, you won't end in them. No matter how many times you struggle, your Savior will bring you through, triumphant.

*Why then,* you may ask, *does Mr. Smith, down the road, have so many overwhelming problems? If you knew them, you'd surely never say that.* Perhaps Mr. Smith is facing those problems but hasn't reached the end yet. God may be beginning His rescue even now, and when it comes, it will be wonderful. In a short while, Mr. Smith won't mind anything he went through, because of the final victory. Or maybe Mr. Smith knows Jesus but hasn't been very faithful. Christians who go their own way can't claim all the benefits of God's love. God doesn't force resistant people to accept His help.

But in the end, whatever today's problem looks like, when we look back from eternity, we'll see the entire plan from God's point of view. Then we'll know the help we waited for came just on time—in God's plan. We'll understand the mysterious troubles that plagued us in life and never seemed to have a point. God promised His rescue, and He will not fail, even if we only comprehend it in eternity.

Need to wait a lifetime to see that salvation? In heaven you'll still vote it was worth every waiting minute.

# WONDERFUL DEED

*We give thanks to you, O God, we give thanks,*
*for your Name is near; men tell of your wonderful deeds.*
Psalm 75:1

Recently my husband and I noticed something odd about our favorite classical music station: They've begun playing Christian music. Not just the standard wordless classics, like Bach, Handel, or Mendelssohn, but hymns. In a metropolitan area that's often resistant to the gospel, it's amazing to be listening, as I write, to "Nearer My God to Thee." We began to wonder if an employee had been converted, but that's not the explanation we got when the selection ended: The hymns we heard influenced a composer they often play.

Still we wonder, because we've heard other Christian music there lately. Perhaps some programmer is a Christian and has found a way to occasionally share God's praise through the selections. We'll probably never know.

When faithful Christians work, they get opportunities to express their thankfulness to God. In an earlier age, men like Bach, Handel, or Mendelssohn testified to their faith by writing works that praised God directly. Not all of us can do that. But we can seek out those chances we have. If we work in a Christian environment or for Christian bosses, we may freely testify to our faith. But if we work for a large, gospel-resistant company, perhaps our praise means requesting that they match our funds for a Christian work instead of a charity that opposes our faith.

What didn't seem like a "wonderful deed" when we heard it on a Christian station is just that in another place. We're glad the message is being told in a different place, to people who would never hear otherwise.

That's just what people who work in a resistant company may be doing. We're glad they're there.

# STANDING FIRM

*"Heaven and earth will pass away,*
*but My words will by no means pass away."*
LUKE 21:33 NKJV

When you read the Bible, is it just words to you? Sometimes we all struggle to keep our attention on the Word, instead of thinking about distractions. But straying minds need to recognize that this Book isn't just a collection of words or sentences. It's the foundation of life. Focusing on biblical truth is important, because nothing in Scripture changes, becomes irrelevant, or leaves us—unlike daily troubles and concerns.

Imagine, Jesus' words are firmer than bedrock. No one can change His mind about anything He said, and He won't go back on a single promise. What Jesus said, He really meant, even after two thousand years. Though times and attitudes alter in this world, for Jesus to change a letter of His speech would be the end of the world, because it would change God's unchanging nature.

At the end of time the mountains and valleys will disappear. Even in our own age they may lose some of their size or be filled in. But Jesus, along with His love and salvation, never differs a bit. That means we can plant our feet completely on Jesus and He'll never heave up beneath us or throw us into a stream. He's reliable because that's His eternal nature. Nothing on earth or in heaven or hell can alter Him by a hairsbreadth.

This is the God in whom we've trusted. Every word He's given us is precious, and we can stand firm in it for eternity.

# JOIN THE PRAISE

*And they worshiped Him, and returned to Jerusalem with great joy,*
*and were continually in the temple praising and blessing God. Amen.*
LUKE 24:52–53 NKJV

B efore His death, when Jesus first spoke of leaving the disciples, they balked at the idea. Doubtless they feared they'd never manage "without" Him. And the days that followed, with His crucifixion and their fears, were certainly hard. But just before the Book of Luke ends, following the Resurrection, we see a wonderful change come over these fearful men. Though Jesus left again, rising to heaven before their eyes, their fear turned to rejoicing.

The difference? He'd shown them, through the Old Testament Scriptures, that He fulfilled the ancient prophecies; He proved He was God. And once they understood the meaning of Jesus' life, death, and resurrection, Jesus gave them a mission: to preach the Good News to all the nations.

Now the Twelve could see the big picture. Where once they'd huddled away in a corner, fearing the Roman authorities, they publicly praised God for all He'd done. They were men with a positive purpose, committed to carrying it out.

Right now, like the disciples, we may feel we miss the "big picture," too. Often we wonder what God has in store, and that questioning may cause doubt to rule our lives, instead of Jesus. But we have seen much the apostles didn't have—ours is the complete New Testament story, including the epistles, and we have seen God's faithfulness to the church for two thousand years.

We know whom we trust in, and His Spirit is ours. Can we do less than join the praise?

119

# BRIMMING WITH HIS SPIRIT

*May you receive more and more of God's mercy, peace, and love.*
JUDE 2 NLT

What a blessing, to continually receive more and more of God's mercy, peace, and love. That's just the kind of Christian life we'd like to have—until we're bursting with these good spiritual experiences, to the point where we simply can't hold them in.

Maybe we have already received so much from God. Our lives have changed drastically because of the salvation He offered. But bursting? Perhaps we wouldn't use *that* word to describe ourselves.

That's because God doesn't overfill us with His blessings. He gives us enough to share, then waits to see what we do with it. Like a good steward, He's not going to splurge with blessings then watch them sit being ignored or only used for personal gain. God gives blessings so we can encourage, teach, and lead others into a relationship with Him. He doesn't give them so that we can bulge with His unused gifts.

But if we receive God's gifts and pass them on to others, take hold of His Word and teachings, and use them to show others how to live, God fills us again. The concept isn't for us to become spiritual gluttons, but for us to be filled, share those benefits, and, as we empty, to allow His Spirit to make us full again.

When we've made that our lifestyle, we are truly blessed—and so are others who come in contact with us. Their growth in turn touches others' lives—and on and on it goes. The joys of mercy, peace, and love abound, just as God planned.

# BLOOD BENEFITS

*When we bless the cup at the Lord's Table,*
*aren't we sharing in the benefits of the blood of Christ?*
*And when we break the loaf of bread,*
*aren't we sharing in the benefits of the body of Christ?*
1 CORINTHIANS 10:16 NLT

First-century pagans got the idea that Christians drank blood and decided they were really a strange group of people. They didn't understand that wine symbolized blood. Modern Christians may not have much more effect on their generation than the Christian Romans, when they try to describe the meaning of communion to unbelievers. Unbelievers just don't get the picture.

No one who fails to understand the sacrifice Jesus made to bring us into fellowship with God has a clear view of what the wine and bread mean. It sounds so harsh, when in reality it is a picture of God's greatest blessing.

But God has shown Christians truths no non-Christian discerns. Jesus gave His life, not just as an ephemeral idea, but in reality for us, personally. What may once have seemed a theological concept that didn't quite touch our lives became concrete when we recognized our sin, offered it to Him for forgiveness, and made Him Lord of all our days. So when Paul speaks of communion, we don't see the blood as much as we see the gift of forgiveness Jesus died to bring.

God only gives His benefits to those who have made that commitment. But understanding Jesus' sacrifice and sitting in church to receive communion are not the only advantages of knowing God. As we asked Him into our lives, He came and began to make it new. We became part of His family—the body of Christ, blessed in every way by Jesus' blood.

Take hold of that blessing today.

# HOMEWARD BOUND

*All praise to him who loves us and has freed us*
*from our sins by shedding his blood for us.*
*He has made us his Kingdom and his priests*
*who serve before God his Father.*
*Give to him everlasting glory!*
*He rules forever and ever! Amen!*

REVELATION 1:5–6 NLT

Jesus' sacrifice freed us from sin. But what we will do with that liberty is up to us. God does not force us to obey; instead, He gives us pictures of His will and the blessings He plans for those who follow Him. Because He loves us, He woos us with the joys He has in store, instead of demanding obedience.

Part of that picture appears here in Revelation, in a praise-filled view of our everlasting destiny. Designed to be in His kingdom, we were saved to serve God eternally by ceaselessly magnifying Him.

Today, earthbound, we begin our praise relationship by using our escape from sin for a good purpose. Giving Him freedom to rule our lives offers us the best liberty possible. As we see His work here on earth, the joy of heaven begins to flood our souls. We build confidence in the delights heaven offers. Who would want to come to God's eternal kingdom feeling as if praising Him were a chore? Perhaps that's why unbelievers never set foot inside. Even if you brought them there, like unwilling church attendees, they'd only desire to leave.

Enjoying the glory in heaven is only for those who delight in it on earth, so let's start singing His song before God calls us home. As we look forward to eternity, praise can radiate from our lips.

# GLAD WORSHIP

*I was glad when they said unto me,*
*Let us go into the house of the LORD.*
PSALM 122:1 KJV

Have you had one of those Sundays when just getting to church was a challenge? Maybe one of your children was sick on Saturday night, and you stayed up too late. Or you got together with friends, and the fellowship was so good you lost track of time; when you got to bed, it was simply too late. Or maybe you're having a challenge with another church member and just don't look forward to seeing that person.

Rolling out of bed in the morning may not be your favorite thing, but don't let that keep you from getting together with your congregation for worship. Don't make a habit of not getting there on time, because even if you're tired, you will miss out on a lot of joy. Avoid church more than once, and you'll probably begin to feel empty or as if you've lost something.

God puts gladness in the human heart at the thought of worshiping Him in the company of other believers. It's a kind of sharing you won't find in the office, with your non-Christian friends, or in a social club. Only a fellowship of believers who share love for God feels the joy David describes here.

If things aren't perfect at your church or you're having a disagreement with someone, don't let it keep you from God's house. After all, you're there to worship Him, not that person. As an added benefit, He might even help you settle your differences peacefully.

# GIFTS FOR ETERNITY

*The generous prosper and are satisfied;*
*those who refresh others will themselves be refreshed.*
PROVERBS 11:25 NLT

God offers Christians this wonderful blessing: Those who give will also receive. Whether it's money, time, energy, or another commodity, spiritual or physical, God does not forget anything we've done. Just like the gift of a cup of cold water that He will see gets its just reward (Matthew 10:42), God never ignores any generous gifts we offer at a price to ourselves.

In a world that tries to hoard time, money, and love, Jesus calls us to do just the opposite. We are to care for those who hurt, lift up those who can't help themselves, and look out for our brothers and sisters. As we do that, we don't lose out, as unbelievers expect. Instead our lives are mysteriously revived and refilled.

Loss is the final reward of those who fear to give. They hold on to their money, but they never have enough, while a generous neighbor prospers, even if she doesn't have a lot of free cash. Others cling tight to their love, rarely sharing it, only to have it slip out of their hands.

Whether or not a person is a Christian, this truth works in each life. Generous unbelievers may benefit from it—at least in this world. Christians who do not learn generosity may enter eternity with little to show for their time on earth.

Want refreshment? Do not hold too tight to the things God loans you for a few decades on earth. Giving allows you to receive not only here, but for eternity.

# GIVING PROMISE

*He that findeth his life shall lose it:*
*and he that loseth his life for my sake shall find it.*
MATTHEW 10:39 KJV

What is life to you? Is it tied up only in your physical being? Or how well you live, either in terms of the affection of others or your standard of living? We all have something we think is important to us—something we'd really regret losing. What if God asked us to let go of it?

Maybe he wouldn't take our spouses away or ask us to live in poverty, but He might ask us to allow our mates the freedom to spend time ministering to others, apart from us. Or He might request that we give some of that income to people in need.

If we hold on tightly to whatever God has given, we risk losing it. A husband whose wife objects to his leadership role in the church may begin to feel distant from her because she thwarted a ministry he felt called to by God. When a well-to-do Christian refuses to aid those whose lives are at risk, she may be surprised to find she doesn't receive an expected bonus in the workplace.

Giving to Jesus, whether it's time, money, or one's physical being, isn't a loss in the end. Though a spouse may miss time with the partner engaged in ministry, other blessings—like spiritual growth that benefits the marriage—may soon appear. The one who provides money to a needy soul could find growth in her spiritual life.

You can't give to God and not be blessed. If you don't feel the blessing this side of heaven, He has stored it up in eternity for you. You've found life in Him that will never end. He promised!

# WHOLE CURE

*He fell face down on the ground at Jesus' feet,*
*thanking him for what he had done.*
*This man was a Samaritan.*
LUKE 17:16 NLT

Jesus healed ten lepers, but only the Samaritan had a tender enough conscience to come back and give thanks. Though the Jews considered his race outcasts, this "unacceptable" man showed a spirit nine of their own people lacked. As we read the story, we begin to wonder: *Why did the other nine fail to come? Had they not received an equal blessing? Did they think they "deserved" what they got?*

Leprosy was a terrible, incurable disease in the first century. To have it meant spending your life as an outcast, so you wouldn't pass it on to others. But the nine didn't connect the comparison between their physical and spiritual conditions. Obviously, this man understood that once he'd been separated from God, and now he had relationship with the Holy One. Not to thank Him would have been unconscionable.

Jesus promised the man his faith had healed him. What of the other nine? Whatever happened to their bodies, their souls certainly lacked closeness to the Savior. All they could pass on to others was information about their brief, seemingly joyless, contact with Jesus.

But the healed man had something other than disease to talk about. He received the body and soul healing only Jesus offers. His faith, the Savior promised, made him whole. Instead of disease, his life, even in this one recorded act, shared the joy of knowing Jesus.

Are we trying to share a joyless faith that's worse than leprosy, or have we experienced the whole healing of Jesus? If our souls have not rejoiced in the Good News, we need to return to the only One who has the cure.

# BLESSED PEACE

*"God blesses those who work for peace,*
*for they will be called the children of God."*
MATTHEW 5:9 NLT

When we think of peace, it's often in connection with an international peace process. But here Jesus isn't only speaking to world leaders. God's peace has a much larger picture, one every Christian takes part in. By bringing the message of the Good News to others, we offer lasting peace to the human heart.

Many churches address this need in many ways. They start by bringing the gospel message to hurting people but don't stop there. After people come to know Jesus, they have not exhausted God's peace. Battles may still rage in their homes. That's why many churches continue bringing peace to struggling families by offering weekend studies or Bible classes that help couples have a better marriage or parents relate better to their children.

God doesn't put a "peace" stamp on our lives the day we commit ourselves to Him. Though our lives improve with that choice, no automatic alteration impacts our families. This verse is right when it says peace—whether between nations or individuals—is work.

But we need not worry. When God gives us a task, He also empowers us to accomplish it. He blesses our efforts, though they may not bear fruit immediately. Even when others ignore our attempts, obedience changes our own lives and improves our Christian walks. We draw closer to God, even if we cannot improve the lives of others.

God doesn't command that we be successful in our peacemaking, though we may be. He only requires us to work at it. Blessings for that obedience will still come from His hand.

# FATHER LOVE

*All praise to the God and Father of our Lord Jesus Christ.*
*He is the source of every mercy and the God who comforts us.*
2 CORINTHIANS 1:3 NLT

New Christians often fall deeply in love with Jesus, but despite their love for the Son, they remain ambivalent about God the Father. They know Jesus—they have seen Him work wonders in their lives, and they have committed completely to Him—but they carry baggage about God the Father that seems to separate them from Him. Based on past experience, they think they see a difference between the two facets of the Godhead.

Often this kind of attitude has more to do with humans than the Father. Perhaps an earthly father wasn't the best example, and the new Christian expects God the Father to act as Daddy did. That expectation drives a wedge between them. Or because a person attended a church that was rule-bound, she expects that God only wants to punish her.

Paul knew better. He understood that whatever Jesus was, God the Father was, too. The believer is not dealing with a good-cop, bad-cop divinity. Both parts of the Godhead have the same goals and methods. Neither is harsh nor wicked; neither wants to manipulate the new Christian. There is no split between the Father, Son, and Spirit.

When we feel mercy and comfort, we shouldn't think it simply comes from Jesus. Everything Jesus does is rooted in the Father. Those gentle blessings are from every portion of the Trinity. When Jesus loves us, so do the Father and Spirit. No person of the Godhead has a different goal.

All praise to the Father. He loves us as much as Jesus does. Let's appreciate Him, too.

# MORNING JOY

*For His anger is but for a moment, His favor is for life;*
*Weeping may endure for a night, But joy comes in the morning.*
PSALM 30:5 NKJV

When God redirects a life, it often causes pain. We humans don't enjoy being told we've headed off in the wrong direction. And if God's redirection means we have to change a habit, we may experience trouble redesigning our lives. We may even ask ourselves if God still loves us.

God reminds us that His anger at sin is only short-term. Like a loving parent, He plans to deal with the problem and move on in love. Correction doesn't last as long as blessing. And though we may resist leaving our wrongdoing behind, He insists on it because He's looking out for our long-term good.

We have a choice—we can keep going our own way or accept the changes God wants to make in our lives. Or to put it another way, we can stay stuck in our own unprofitable spot or learn a new way that will bring us blessings.

Though we may suffer for a short time, as we submit to God instead of resisting His Spirit, we receive joy and a new lifestyle that benefits us for years—and eternity. Whether the suffering lasts for one dark night, as we agonize over a simple problem, or clings for years, we can be certain joy will follow. Even if we never see the greatest benefit on earth, we can count on rejoicing in eternity. In that forever morning, we'll praise the Father who gave brief pain but everlasting joy.

# ESCAPE ROUTE

*Praise be to the LORD, for he showed his wonderful love to me
when I was in a besieged city.*

PSALM 31:21

David knew what it meant to be surrounded by his enemies.
Though God anointed him king of Israel, rebellious King Saul
had another idea. For years he hunted David mercilessly, to keep the
younger man from taking his throne.

Yet even David's worst military problem, facing death inside a
besieged city, was God's opportunity. Through all the dangers and
fears, God's king learned what it meant to trust in his Savior. Without
God at his side, David understood he would never stay alive, much
less sit on a throne.

We may never know what it means to lie inside a war-torn city or
have a ruler determined to take our lives, but like David, we have been
besieged by sin. Though God described David as a man after His own
heart (1 Samuel 13:14), the king was far from perfect. When David
erred, he sinned impressively—committing murder and adultery.

Even then, God showed the king His wonderful love. The
prophet Nathan confronted the king, showing the Lord's displeasure.
David accepted his own wrongdoing, and his heart turned away from
it as God showed him his error and gave him forgiveness. Wonderful
love flooded the king's spirit and brought him to obedience for the
rest of his life.

When sin besieges us, God always offers us an alternative. Escape
from the city of evil lies right before us, when we follow His path out
of destruction. Like David, are we willing to take Jesus' forgiveness
escape route?

# SUCCESS PRINCIPLES

*"This book of the law shall not depart from your mouth,*
*but you shall meditate on it day and night,*
*so that you may be careful to do according to all that is written in it;*
*for then you will make your way prosperous,*
*and then you will have success."*

JOSHUA 1:8 NASB

M any business people attribute their success to the truths they've learned in the Bible. And if you run a business by following scriptural truths, you may well lead effectively. But when this verse talks about prosperity and success, it's not simply referring to financial or business success. Joshua wasn't really concerned about either. But he did have a mission—to bring God's people into the Promised Land.

Once they got there, the people could choose to live as God commanded or take their beautiful surroundings for granted. If they remembered their past and lived by the law Moses brought to them, God would make them successful—their harvests would overflow. But how much grain they raised or how many animals filled their fields was not the best prosperity the Israelites could have. It might come as the result of an intimate relationship with God, but it couldn't replace that fellowship.

You've seen people with millions—or even billions—of dollars who have material prosperity but don't seem happy. They can buy everything they want, but they don't relate well to a spouse or raise happy children. But some people who barely cover their expenses have the same problems.

The answer, no matter how much cash you have, remains the same. Truly successful relationships are based on God. Those who know the Word, follow God faithfully, and live what He has taught them won't have perfect lives, but they can develop increasingly better ones as they follow the guidelines of the Master.

# HEART JOY

*With joy you will draw water from the wells of salvation.*
ISAIAH 12:3

Being saved is a wonderful thing. No matter how many secular cartoons portray it mockingly, no matter how many non-Christians make fun of it, no one can destroy the joy that wells up from knowing Jesus.

People who don't know Him don't have a well. Their lives are dry and empty, compared to faithful Christians' lives. They may be good at covering up that fact with a smile or jokes, but deep inside their hearts is what St. Augustine described as a "God-shaped hole." Though they may have trouble clearly identifying it, something is missing. A vague feeling that there may be something more to life plagues some nonbelievers, but the solution to the problem evades them.

One day, God reaches into that unsuspecting heart. Unexpectedly, the joy begins as the Spirit begins cleansing sin.

That water of salvation doesn't come from a fountain, but a well. It won't automatically flow into our lives, whether or not we desire it. Christian growth doesn't happen without our will. We must draw it up in our lives, making the effort to bring it from the deep places.

Yet this effort is not drudgery, if we hunger to commune with the Savior. Reading the Scripture and speaking with Him in prayer feed the empty heart. The effort of coming to Him and learning more of His nature brings more delight for the faithful student of God.

Have you recognized the hole in your heart and come to the Savior for filling? If so, you'll rejoice at Jesus' name and keep it forever on your tongue.

# UNCHANGEABLE

*"I am the LORD, and I do not change.*
*That is why you descendants of Jacob*
*are not already completely destroyed."*
MALACHI 3:6 NLT

Listen to any two pollster's results, and you'll begin to wonder if people either don't know what they believe or don't tell the truth about it twice in a row. But in fact, people have very changeable minds. Media coverage may influence them, or a friend may speak persuasively and alter the direction of their thinking. Or they may be confused about an issue.

None of that is true of our Creator. Only God doesn't change His opinion and always knows what to think. When He says something, He means it.

That's good, because with the disobedience He's had from humans—both Jacob's descendants, whom Malachi spoke to, and today's believers—changing His mind might seem like a good idea. If He'd been a more mutable God, He might have immediately given up on people instead of sending Jesus to save us.

Though we may feel tempted to ignore this verse because it talks about destruction, or we may want to object because it seems like a threat from God, it's neither of those things. Actually this is a positive statement. God reminds us that He *could* have destroyed us all, because we sin. We're guilty as charged. None of us have never disobeyed God. Even after we accept His grace, our struggle with sin remains. So when God explains that He could have changed but didn't, it's reason to rejoice.

We should praise God because He doesn't need a pollster to make a choice, isn't influenced even by the best arguments or our worst actions. God is faithful to Himself and doesn't alter. Let's rejoice.

# ROAR WITH JOY

*Let the sea roar, and all its fullness;*
*Let the field rejoice, and all that is in it.*
*Then the trees of the woods shall rejoice before the LORD,*
*For He is coming to judge the earth.*

1 CHRONICLES 16:32–33 NKJV

One day, the world, right down to the oceans and fields, will rejoice in Jesus. On the day He judges the earth, people who don't know Him may gnash their teeth, but all believers and the earth itself will begin a joyfest.

When God judges, He will hardly tell a tree that it's sinned or a field that it didn't do the best it could with its life. We understand that innately. But once God judges His human creations and sets all right, the sea, fields, and forests will be changed to an eternally perfect state. At His appearing, the world will be truly recycled—made anew the way it should be.

Like the earth, we Christians rejoice at the idea that Jesus will come. It isn't simply so that a wicked neighbor will get his comeuppance. We look forward to His redesigning our lives, just as He will remake the world, removing the spiritual pollution and results of unwise choices from our hearts. Though we've already begun to experience God's changes in our souls, one day everything about us will be made new in Him. No longer will sin tempt or wicked people seek to derail us. The world—including us—will be spanking clean, ready to worship the Creator.

That's something to roar with joy about!

# OPENING EARS AND EYES

*In that day the deaf shall hear the words of the book,*
*And the eyes of the blind shall see out of obscurity and out of darkness.*
ISAIAH 29:18 NKJV

Can you imagine being unable to hear or see? That's the way God describes people who don't know Him. Like those whose faculties don't work properly, nonbelievers simply can't communicate with Him or understand what He is. He's a closed book to them—one they can't even begin to read.

It was like that for us. Once, before He came into our lives, we were locked away from Him by our own sin, unable to comprehend anything about Him. But just as Isaiah prophesied that a day would come when He would break through Israel's stubborn disobedience, and they would again know Him, God reaches out to people today. Never in history has there been a time when He did not open spiritual eyes and ears, though many in Israel have not accepted Him. But someday, like a flood, many of His chosen race will comprehend all He has for them.

When we reach out in faith to someone and don't get a positive response, do we recognize that we're speaking to a spiritually deaf soul? When we do something kind and get criticism in return, do we understand we're in contact with a blind heart? Though we're tempted to shut up or respond in anger, we cannot spread the gospel by having a short fuse. Satan has deafened and blinded all humanity, and apart from the Holy Spirit's work, none of us can see or hear.

Kindness in the face of opposition may begin the work that opens deaf ears and lightens blind eyes. Let's start to unclog ears and lighten the darkness.

# ETERNAL HOME

*"Sing and rejoice, O daughter of Zion!*
*For behold, I am coming and I will dwell in your midst," says the LORD.*
ZECHARIAH 2:10 NKJV

What joy it will be to live with God directly beside us. We look forward to a day when He will walk among His believers (Leviticus 26:12). Though Jesus spent a few years on earth with His disciples and reflected God's glory here, that wasn't the only time God wanted to spend with His people. In eternity, He will be right nearby us. We won't have to travel or search for Him. God plans on dwelling with us (Revelation 21:3).

Today, our connection with God can seem distant because He's not physically present. It's easy to stray when we feel as if He is "up" in heaven and we are here "below." We struggle to understand His will and please Him. But one day it will not be so.

If we knew God were coming to live with us, what would we change? Maybe we'd want to fix up our house. The peeling paint wouldn't be good enough for the Lord of glory. And maybe we'd have to rebuild some of the structure, so it wouldn't sag any longer. If Jesus had to step on floorboards that bowed and creaked, we'd be filled with embarrassment.

Of course, we won't have Jesus corporeally in our earthly abodes. He plans instead to bring us to live in His heaven. But, just as with our earthly home, the soul that arrives there can be an embarrassment or a blessing. When God's judgment comes, will it show up only flaws or reflect a faithful obedience? Which kind of soul will be revealed, when we reach our eternal home?

# DADDY GOD

*And because you are sons,*
*God has sent forth the Spirit of His Son into your hearts,*
*crying out, "Abba, Father!"*
GALATIANS 4:6 NKJV

You are God's child. That might seem a rather ordinary thing, but consider it more carefully, and feel the amazement of that truth. The Creator of the universe, the all-powerful God, who didn't even begin to wear Himself out making our world, much less the universe, wants to be your daddy (after all, that's what *abba* means). This awesome being wants you to come to Him as a young child who trusts Him and seeks His love and protection.

Nothing that happens is beyond the Lord's domain. Nothing can touch us that the heavenly Father can't deal with, and no event can ruin His plan for good in our lives. All things, He promises, will work together for our good, if we love Him (Romans 8:28).

God didn't simply have the prophets write down the Bible and leave us to figure His love out for ourselves. He actually put part of Himself in our hearts when we accepted the sacrifice of His Son— the Spirit entered us in a moment, and He hasn't left since, even when we've ignored Him and denied His work in our lives.

Like a daddy, God never gives up on us, even in our disobedience. But just because He did forgive, we can't take advantage by forgetting He is still Lord of the universe and treating Him without respect. Because He loved us, He did not hold the sin against us, but our Lord is no wimp. He disciplines unrepentant children. If He didn't do that, He wouldn't be our daddy.

# TRUE LIBERTY

*Stand fast therefore in the liberty by which Christ has made us free,*
*and do not be entangled again with a yoke of bondage.*
GALATIANS 5:1 NKJV

Jesus made you free! Do you really believe it? Or have you allowed Satan to whisper in your ear that you'll really be free, if you can just get one thing right?

Christians aren't immune to Satan's lies that we have to do something to reach heaven, and some become completely entangled, seriously compromising their Christian life and testimony with their perfectionistic replacements for faith. Jesus made them free, yet they don't live in liberty. They've missed the truth that Christian freedom recognizes that faith in God alone saves, instead of trying to earn our way into heaven.

Teachings that purport to be Christian and aren't, or well-meaning "Christian rules" that distort God's Word, can distract Christians from the real liberation God offers. That's the kind of thing the false teachers in Galatia were telling faithful Christians. They wanted to add circumcision to God's message to New Testament believers.

God doesn't put anyone into bondage. Legalistic rules or rites that purport to save aren't part of His plan. That's where many Jews of Paul's day had gone wrong. They had a gazillion rules to follow but lacked a faith relationship with God.

Many religions try to earn their way into a heavenly kingdom. People don't like to accept the truth that no act we perform on earth can get us there. They want to "do" something to achieve heaven and resist God's grace-filled forgiveness that requires only an open heart.

We can't merit heaven, but we can make it our eternal destiny. We must accept that He alone makes us free. Then we are free indeed.

# HEAVENLY PLACES

*But God, who is rich in mercy. . .raised us up together,*
*and made us sit together in the heavenly places in Christ Jesus.*
EPHESIANS 2:4, 6 NKJV

A heavenly place awaits every Christian, a spot in heaven with Jesus, where we can experience every good thing in the eternal joy of the Father.

When we talk about being in glory with Jesus, do we take it lightly? Do we assume we're going to be there because we somehow deserve it? Hardly. On our own, we'd never reach heaven. Even if we filled our lives with good works, we'd never become holy. Only God can make that change in our lives, when we trust in the work of His Son, Jesus.

But God, in His mercy, offers us the ability to spend eternity with Him, not in a little hole of a place or in the worst corner of His kingdom or down the street from the best place in town. Instead He gives us the prime spot, with His Son, Jesus.

Knowing the blessing that lies before us should humble our hearts. Because we know our eternal, royal destiny, we must follow our Savior's path and seek to show all those who have never received mercy the rich blessings that lie before them, if only they accept the sacrifice of God's only begotten Son.

No spot in eternity exists for those who assume they are better than others, because God graciously offered them this gift. The Father offers no room to the proud and disdainful. So let's start living today as we plan to spend our eternity, as children of the merciful King. He gave us life in heavenly places; can we do any less than model that joyful message?

# BEYOND THE BLESSING

*"If you keep quiet at a time like this,*
*deliverance for the Jews will arise from some other place,*
*but you and your relatives will die. What's more, who can say but that*
*you have been elevated to the palace for just such a time as this?"*
ESTHER 4:14 NLT

When her cousin Mordecai asked Esther to stand up for her people, the queen had a lot to lose. Her husband had already gotten rid of one queen who displeased him, and this young, beautiful woman could even lose her life. Yet after Mordecai reminded her that God was still in control, she approached the king about the wrongdoing of his favorite, Haman, and ended up saving her people. The king entirely supported her.

Like Esther, we find ourselves in difficult situations. We may not be threatened with loss of life or position, but maybe it's a job or promotion we'll have to bypass. Perhaps we fear that we'll ruin a relationship that may be rocky, but at least exists; we'd prefer not to lose it entirely.

But when God places a challenge before us, it's never because He plans on deserting us. As with Esther, He may open the ears of those who listen to our plight. Or if they won't listen, He provides an even better workplace or friendship. Nothing that we lose because we obey God will ruin our lives.

God's still in control of every situation, every emotion, and every human thought. The universe belongs to Him, including all the people in it. At such a time as this, He may be planning something wonderful, a step beyond the problem. Just because we don't see the blessing yet doesn't mean it isn't on its way.

# DRIVING WIND

*"But suddenly, your ruthless enemies will be driven away
like chaff before the wind."*
ISAIAH 29:5 NLT

All sorts of dangerous enemies on the horizon strike fear into our hearts. Whether it's a person we'd rather not face, the loss of a loved one, or a lifelong problem, we'd like to see them suddenly disappear. Like chaff being tossed up into the air by a farmer and disappearing from his crop, we'd like to believe they'll depart from our lives.

God promised to remove Jerusalem's enemies this way. One day, far in the future, their adversaries would become nothing more than debris, driven on the wind. But first, God planned to bring His disobedient people low. When they reached the edge of death and recognized their neediness, He promised to come in like a driving wind and clean all the confusion from their lives.

If we're in situations that feel like spiritual or physical death and need that driving wind, God offers us a similar help. But the blessing will not come to those who have their own proud plan or solution to the problem. When our faces are in the dust, and we recognize no other God than the Lord, He answers our need, whether it's with wind, an army, or simply a touch of love.

No enemy stands before God. So if we're still facing a problem, we have to ask why. Are we standing in our own pride, or is it something God is leading us through for our own benefit?

But when God commands our enemies to depart, they'll be gone in a moment, and no one will find them floating on the wind. Then our thanks will reach up to God as we praise His works again.

# GUARDED BY GOD

*But the Lord is faithful,*
*who will establish you and guard you from the evil one.*
2 THESSALONIANS 3:3 NKJV

Many years ago, I went on a job interview. The position looked good, and I was called in for a second interview, but someone else ended up getting the position. For awhile, I wondered what had happened. What had I done wrong?

Later, I realized that maybe I hadn't done anything wrong—maybe what I had *been* was "wrong." Naively I hadn't realized that as a Christian, I would have had conflicts with the kind of books I'd be working with. Daily I would have had to read things that went counter to my faith. Instead of denying me a good thing, God had been protecting me from something really wrong. He was guarding me from the evil one. Finally, I was glad I hadn't gotten what once seemed like a wonderful spot.

God faithfully looks out for us, even when we aren't aware of problems. Instead of letting us innocently fall into trouble, He goes before us and paves the way to our making the right decision, as long as we're honestly trying to follow His will.

You've probably seen the same kind of thing in your life: the person you thought you wanted to marry, but didn't, and later found out something that made you realize why God didn't let it happen; or the move you wanted to make that stalled out, and when you found out why, that delay made you happy.

God looks ahead for you and establishes you in His blessings. As long as you follow His will and ask to walk in His way, you won't go wrong.

# THE WORD'S WORTH

*All Scripture is given by inspiration of God,*
*and is profitable for doctrine, for reproof, for correction,*
*for instruction in righteousness, that the man of God may be complete,*
*thoroughly equipped for every good work.*
2 TIMOTHY 3:16–17 NKJV

Most nonbelievers run life by their own rules. That's a recipe for disaster, since it leads to mistakes, wrong ideas, and troubles. But because they don't have a life direction, it's the best they can do. The Bible condemns this attitude when it talks about people doing what is right in their own eyes. Proverbs 12:15 describes such a person as a fool, and Psalm 14:1 defines a fool as one who does not believe in Him.

But God won't leave the Christian at such a loss. He wants His people to know where they are going and be able to turn aside from wrong. Therefore, He gave us extensive directions that show us right from wrong and how we can best serve Him and live in an upright way. When we're focused on these truths, He says we're complete to do good works.

But God also leaves it up to us. We can read His Word, or we can ignore it. He won't strong-arm us to pick up a Bible or follow what we read there. He'd rather have willing followers who have experienced the joy of knowing Him and walking in His way.

But making use of all God has offered us, learning about Him, and putting His Word into action will never lead to disaster. Though trials and troubles come, they turn to good in His hands. Who could run his or her own life that way, without the Word?

# WALKING IN TRUTH

*I rejoiced greatly that I have found some of your children walking in truth, as we received commandment from the Father.*

2 JOHN 4 NKJV

What a joy for any pastor or teacher—whether it's John, who wrote these words, or today's church leaders who hear them—to know the faith lessons shared with congregants or students are being received and used. After all, good leaders don't talk in order to hear their own voices. If that were all it was, most would feel they had a better use for their time and energies. No one wants to deliver a sermon or lesson plan that no one really listens to.

John expressed his appreciation for the children of the "elect lady" (2 John 1 KJV) who had really heard the gospel message he'd received from the Lord. They'd made it part of their lifestyle. Doubtless their words, actions, and thoughts, influenced by the apostle's teaching, shone with the light of the gospel's truth.

But note that only some of the children walked in God's truth. Any church leader has run into the believers who show up every Sunday morning, but by Monday it's apparent the truth they heard the day before meant little to them. While their siblings who listened brought joy, these disobedient souls hurt the heart of that faithful leader.

When the leaders of your church think of you, do they rejoice or feel pain? If they've faithfully preached the good news, have you listened and made use of it in your life? Have you thanked them for their part in God's touch on your life, as you've heard the message of Jesus? It's not too late to do that now.

# MIGHTY ONE

*It is the same way for the resurrection of the dead.*
*Our earthly bodies, which die and decay,*
*will be different when they are resurrected, for they will never die.*
*Our bodies now disappoint us, but when they are raised,*
*they will be full of glory.*
*They are weak now, but when they are raised,*
*they will be full of power.*
1 CORINTHIANS 15:42–43 NLT

"Death be not proud," seventeenth-century poet John Donne wrote, "though some have called thee Mighty and dreadful, for thou art not so, For those whom thou think'st thou dost overthrow, Die not, poor death, nor yet canst thou kill me." When the cleric-poet penned those words, he must have been thinking of these verses that promise not just spiritual, but physical life in eternity.

Death, Donne reminds us in his verse, is not the final say. Though Satan may rule for awhile on earth, God remains in control. In His own time, He makes it apparent that those with faith in Him may lose life here on earth, but they gain eternity.

Though our bodies seem strong now, Paul reminds us that in reality, they are very weak. Disease overtakes us in a moment, accidents may kill in a minute. We fear death because we shrink at the separation from loved ones it brings. Perhaps we also dread the unknown we go into, though we believe in the One in command of it.

Yet as the apostle and Donne make clear, we need not fear this death, because by God's grace, eternity is ours. In the endless time of praise that lies before us, we will be filled with His power. God is the truly mighty One, and our trust lies wholly in Him.

# SECOND-HALF BLESSING

*So the LORD blessed Job in the second half of his life*
*even more than in the beginning.*
JOB 42:12 NLT

Our youth-loving society praises those with few years and great beauty. But it ignores what Victorian Robert Browning called "the last of life for which the first was made." About a hundred years after Browning lived, we try to avoid thoughts of life after forty. Surely the first half of life is the most blessed, we tend to believe.

For Job—and many others—that is not true. Job wrestled with his loss of home, family, and friends in the first half of life but saw incredible blessing after he'd overcome through God's grace. Though he probably mourned those lost children long afterward, he could not complain over lost herds or goods. God gave him even more once he knew Him more intimately. And though the children could never be replaced, God gave him sons and daughters again. According to Scripture, his later days were even better than the first.

When the world tempts us to feel life has passed us by, let's remember we aren't finished yet. God may give us many wonderful relationships, increased spiritual growth, and physical blessings in the years ahead. Until our very last day on earth, the Savior is not done giving us good things. As long as He has a purpose for us here, He supports us in many ways.

So instead of feeling sorry for ourselves or toting up the days, months, weeks, and years that are already past, let's praise Him for all the benefits He's already given and look forward to all those that may lie ahead. As Browning also said, "The best is yet to be."

# PRAISE PARTY

*We wait for the blessed hope—the glorious appearing*
*of our great God and Savior, Jesus Christ.*
TITUS 2:13

If you had to describe your greatest hope in the Christian life, what would it be? Salvation and life with Jesus in eternity? The hope that God will deal with a problem you face with a loved one? There is one greater hope, and God offers it to all His people.

One day, unexpectedly, Jesus will return. Then all who have trusted Him with their earthly lives will rejoice as they see their faith fulfilled. As our heavenly future appears before us, we will delight in God's faithfulness and begin to receive the reward He promised—to be forever with Him.

Even now, when we think of that day, our hearts lift up in response. Hope and expectation build in our hearts as we desire Him to complete the work He's begun. Excitement for the coming of Jesus is a Christian's hopeful prerogative.

But that great, overwhelming joy won't be for everyone. When Jesus appears, no unbeliever will see a humble carpenter, but all will recognize the glorious King. No one will push Him aside. Suddenly your coworker who made fun of your faith will realize you weren't the one on the wrong track. Those who refused your testimony will understand why you persisted in telling them about Jesus.

When life seems hard and our testimonies fall on hard hearts, may the hope of Jesus never leave us. Because the prospect He offers isn't only for eternity. Today, He softens hard hearts and opens lives to their need for His love. One day, as He appears, that soul we labored to win may lift up His name in praise.

# REFUGE

*Trust in Him at all times, you people;*
*Pour out your heart before Him; God is a refuge for us.*
PSALM 62:8 NKJV

Last night, I woke up and had some trouble getting back to sleep. A second war with Iraq has just begun, and tensions run high in our country. Even the wisest pundits cannot predict the outcome, and politicians speak guardedly. No one can tell what the future holds.

When sleep escapes me, it's easy to start pondering the world scene and wondering what will happen. The media's feeding frenzy could feed my imagination and keep me sleepless for many nights, but it won't. I have a better plan—prayer—and from past experience I know it won't fail me.

Leaders may try to do their best, and I trust they will. But they are only human. None can fully understand all that goes on in our complex world or predict how others will act or where they will be at key moments. So I don't trust much in people. Yet God knows all those things. He sees the beginning from the end (Isaiah 46:10) and will never lose control of this world, no matter what happens.

Since He encourages me to pour out my heart at all times, even during the bad moments, and nothing I can tell Him will be too hard for Him, I'll turn to Him instead. When I wake in the night and pray, He comforts my heart. Though I may not know the end of this war from the beginning, I know who is in charge of the world, and I trust in Him. Like a blanket, I draw God's solace about me and drift off to sleep.

His refuge is more than any blanket—it covers each believer with peace.

# HELP IN NEED

*For I can do everything with the help of Christ*
*who gives me the strength I need.*
PHILIPPIANS 4:13 NLT

I s there something you could do that God would refuse to help you with? No, not as long as you're tapped in to Him and seeking to obey His will.

Of course, that doesn't mean He'll assist you in sin. Don't even think of looking for His help in anything dishonest or that's designed to hurt other people, because it won't be forthcoming. This verse isn't the blanket statement some folks would like to think it is.

Even for faithful Christians, this statement isn't simply a "do as you please" one. Read the context of this passage and you'll see Paul's talking about the way God helped Him through financial difficulties. The Philippians came to his aid when no one else would, and the apostle appreciated it. Though he'd steeled himself to live with nothing but the barest necessities, God's method of providing for him, by the generous act of these believers, made that a thing of the past. God's ways were even better than Paul expected.

God will also give us more than we expect. When no one wants to help, He'll keep us on course with His task for us, even when it's hard. But as we faithfully respond to Him, He may provide unexpected blessings for us that amaze us. Like Paul, we may find ourselves saying, "You didn't have to, but I sure do appreciate it."

God's help often comes through others. Like Paul, let's not forget to give a thank-you to a faithful supporter. God helped us do all with His support, even if it came from another Christian.

# IT'S TAKEN CARE OF

*And this same God who takes care of me*
*will supply all your needs from his glorious riches,*
*which have been given to us in Christ Jesus.*
PHILIPPIANS 4:19 NLT

When God took care of Paul through the Philippians' giving, He did it abundantly. They offered a sacrificial gift, not one that came out of their extra funds. So in turn Paul expressed concern for the Philippians' needs. He thought of the generosity of their hearts and hoped it wouldn't harm them.

But Paul also knew the God they'd obeyed when they offered this gift to him. The apostle had lived with faith in Jesus for many years, through many trials, and had never seen Him fail. Though he'd experienced times of famine and times of great financial blessing, he saw both in the light of the Savior's riches.

Sometimes the riches God offers are those of trust. If you've been in a situation where money was tight and God pulled through for you, you've appreciated the richness of His love. Money never feels as blessed as when God works things out unexpectedly. When you've managed to cover your monthly bills despite a financial disaster that loomed before you, you have experienced praise.

But financial blessings aren't all God offers. Paul promises Jesus will supply every need. Though he'd suffered persecution, gone hungry, been beaten, and felt the loneliness of being the only believer in town, God had never let the apostle down. It's the same for us. Jesus has it all covered—our physical, spiritual, and emotional needs, along with any other we could think of.

Jesus takes care of every part of our lives. All we must do is offer them to Him.

# GOING PLACES

*"Be strong and of good courage, do not fear nor be afraid of them;*
*for the LORD your God, He is the One who goes with you.*
*He will not leave you nor forsake you."*
DEUTERONOMY 31:6 NKJV

Joshua faced a task large enough to daunt anyone: the military might of the nations that already lived in the Promised Land. God had commanded His people to invade and displace these pagan peoples. Not only that, Moses, who had led the people to the new land, had just announced he would not be going with them. His life would end on the wrong side of the Jordan River.

God knew that all His people—including the new leader, Joshua—needed encouragement. So through Moses, He reminded them that He was still in control. Just because they crossed a river, God would not forget them or walk away in another direction.

God made that promise to His people, and He hasn't changed His mind. The promise to protect remains as valid today as it was thousands of years ago. Whether we're moving into new territory or starting a new ministry, He is at our sides. If we marry, have a new baby, or care for an elderly parent, He remains by the side of those who love Him.

You can't take on something new and not have Jesus by your side, unless you're getting into sin. Even then, when you recognize that wrong and turn to Him, He'll be next to you, helping you change your life.

Don't go anywhere without Jesus. You don't need to.

# HEART CHANGE

*But He said,*
*"The things which are impossible with men are possible with God."*
LUKE 18:27 NKJV

Have you got a family member who hasn't accepted Jesus? Are you ready to give up on sharing your faith with this stubborn one?

It's true, people can be stubborn when it comes to refusing to accept Jesus. Even Jesus commented on this when the rich young ruler held on to his riches and self-righteousness instead of following Him.

We can stress and strain over friends or family members and still see them go in the opposite direction. All our efforts to be faithful can seem to end in disappointment. But when that happens, we need to take stock of the situation. Jesus told the disciples it was easier for a camel to go through the eye of a needle than for a rich man to be saved. So they asked who could be saved. This verse gives us His response.

We can't save anyone. No one comes to God because we do all the right things, say all the right words, or give them the right books by the best apologists. All those things may help, of course, but no one comes to God because another has witnessed "perfectly." If that were so, every apologist would boast that his or her entire family was saved. It isn't necessarily so.

What does save people is God's grace. We can pray that a parent's heart will be softened or that a friend will understand what being a Christian means. But we can't make anyone come to Him. Only the Spirit effects the change we seek.

But we can always pray. The Spirit still responds to prayer and touches even the hardest hearts.

# PEACE IN PRAYER

*Be anxious for nothing, but in everything by prayer and supplication,*
*with thanksgiving, let your requests be made known to God.*
PHILIPPIANS 4:6 NKJV

God doesn't want us to worry, get stressed out or bothered. So He offers a solution to those states of mind: prayer. Nothing in this world is beyond His control, He reminds us—there's nothing He won't be happy to help us with, if only we mention it to Him.

So why stick to our own worrywart tendencies or attempt to find other ways around the problem? Maybe we think we don't need to bother God with something "this small." He'd be glad to help with anything, even the tiniest problem. Nothing is below the notice of Him who created subatomic particles. Or maybe we figure we don't need help on this one. He'll be there to share the good things, and if an unexpected trouble comes up, He'll be happy to assist us, too.

God's trying to tell us He wants to be a part of every moment of our lives. Whether it's something we simply need to mention or a deep concern we petition for a long time, He's interested.

Only when we give Him all our anxieties can He have the kind of impact on our lives—and on the lives of others to whom we minister—He's always had in mind. Then we'll also experience two unexpected benefits: thanksgiving and peace. We'll appreciate what our Savior begins to give and offer Him thanks, deepening and expanding our trust relationship. As we do that, harmony will fill our lives.

Find peace in prayer today.

# PROMISE FULFILLED

*And the peace of God, which surpasses all understanding,*
*will guard your hearts and minds through Christ Jesus.*
PHILIPPIANS 4:7 NKJV

If God gives peace, why don't all Christians experience it? Does He save it for some and deny it to others?

No, God offers peace to all His children. But to understand this verse, you can't take it out of context. The verse before this told us not to be anxious but to bring all our concerns to God in prayer. Prayer builds a relationship with the Savior, and the knowledge that God is in control of any trouble in our lives fosters peace in our hearts.

When you see a Christian who lacks peace, though, don't jump to judgment. Maybe the struggle he's dealing with is difficult, and he's given it to God but hasn't seen the results yet. The challenge before him is new, and he's praying hard but struggles with faith. Come alongside such a brother and encourage him that God will see him through. Or maybe she's living on a small paycheck and fears her children will lack something because she can't provide. Remind her that all provision comes from God, who has not given up on her, even if she hasn't seen it yet.

If you have years of faithful service to God at your back, you've been through such challenges and have seen the loyalty of your Savior. You can testify to another that His peace will come, and the promises will be fulfilled. So share that with struggling Christians who have committed their lives to Him but cannot see what He will do. Tell them God's faithfulness is not just for you, but for all who stand firm.

Then pray for that standing-firm believer, and watch that fulfilled promise appear.

# STAINLESS

*"Come now, and let us reason together," says the* LORD,
*"Though your sins are like scarlet,*
*They shall be as white as snow;*
*Though they are red like crimson, they shall be as wool."*
ISAIAH 1:18 NKJV

Anyone who runs a household can tell you how hard stains are to remove from clothing, pots and pans, or a carpet. Unless you use the right cleanser, a stain can remain for the rest of that object's life or may even cause you to throw it away. Stains can be serious business.

Household objects aren't the only things with stains, the Bible tells us. We have one that's hard to remove, too: sin. We may have tried to get it out by focusing on good works, but our best efforts have proved less than successful. It's like taking a deep, dried-in stain and running water on it—it might move it around a bit, but it's unlikely to eradicate the blot.

We may shove our stain about a bit—often expanding it with our good intentions to improve ourselves—but we can't escape it entirely. Sin removal is beyond the ability of any mere human. We can't perform a "sin-ectomy."

But God can get rid of sin. He covers our scarlet sins with the even deeper red of His Son's blood. Miraculously, they turn pure white, like dark ground covered with new snowfall. Where once we could only see the scars of sin, healing begins. Our aching hearts are covered with the cool, healing touch of a Savior whose balm reaches the deepest soul places.

The change has begun. In eternity we'll see what God now sees— ourselves entirely cleansed by the Son, who made us stainless with His sacrifice.

# GOD POWERED

*His divine power has given us everything we need for life*
*and godliness through our knowledge of him who called us*
*by his own glory and goodness.*
2 PETER 1:3

Have you had a day when you felt you were an awful Christian? Maybe you thought you'd let God down so much that He'd never want to connect with you again. As embarrassment covered you, you didn't feel as if you could honestly call yourself a Christian before the world.

On that kind of spectacularly bad day, take heart. God has given you everything you need to be righteous, and He isn't planning on taking it away. He isn't looking to get rid of you or demand your resignation as a Christian. Maybe that's because He didn't expect you to be perfect on your own in the first place. He promised to give you all that you needed to please Him, but not simply through your own effort.

We have all we need for the godly life because God is glorious and good, not because we are. We're not trying to become little gods, but to live daily in the power of His Spirit, which He's already given to us. Because His Spirit fills our souls, we can be cleansed, redirected, and serve our Lord.

So the next time you have a bad day, remember, you're not doing this in your power, but His. Ask Him to cleanse you of all sin, show you the way you need to go, and start walking. Then remember you're heading toward His glory and goodness. Nothing can stop you now.

# UNFAILING CARE

*His compassions fail not.*
*They are new every morning;*
*Great is Your faithfulness.*
LAMENTATIONS 3:22–23 NKJV

When trouble hits, people often start asking questions. *Where is God?* they wonder when a family member becomes seriously ill or a war starts.

It's normal to feel confusion for awhile when you're hit with large problems. Getting it together mentally may take a bit of thinking and praying. But as you enter that time of confusion, be sure of one thing: God has not deserted you. As you wake to a new day of doubt and questioning, His new compassions are ready to meet you. They cannot disappear or fail you, because He promised they will be there, and for that not to be true would mean that God became faithless.

God's faithful nature never changes—if it did, He would not be the immutable One. Imagine if God did vary: He would have given the Bible, then changed His mind about what He said. Then we'd have to have multiple revisions, based on new revelations. What confusion that would lead to, because we'd never know whom to believe. Every person who claimed to have a new view of God could be right.

But God doesn't alter. What He was when the prophet Jeremiah wrote down these words is what He still is. Not a word of Scripture has changed since He first inspired it—the story of His faithfulness remains the same from age to age. He has been there for all believers through the ages.

If we don't see His compassions, perhaps we've been blinded by our situation. But no event on earth changes His tender care for us. All we need is trusting faith that He will never fail. And He won't.

# PATIENT WAITING

*The LORD is good to those who wait for Him,*
*To the soul who seeks Him.*
LAMENTATIONS 3:25 NKJV

None of us gets every expectation fulfilled by God in a moment. All of us wait on Him at times that may seem painful or inconvenient to us. But as we're waiting, do we understand that this, too, can be God's goodness?

Waiting to find a mate can be difficult—I know that from experience. But I decided that marrying the right person—God's person— was better than suffering through a divorce with the wrong person. And wait I did. How long? Let's just put it this way: Anyone who feels that waiting until twenty-five to marry is too long just hasn't begun to wait, if that's God's will.

As the years went by, I was tempted to think I'd done something wrong. I wondered if I had some huge character flaw that no one was willing to share with me. One older friend asked if all the men in my state were blind. Still I waited, patiently praying, seeking to obey God's will for my work and spiritual life. When my social life seemed empty, I still hung on.

Finally, about the time I decided no one was coming, I met my husband, who had also been faithfully waiting. We didn't marry at the usual age but in God's perfect timing. Many problems that might have endangered our relationship, if we'd married earlier, had already been dealt with. God had been good to us, though we hadn't understood it all those years.

If you, too, are waiting on God's timing, do so patiently. Trust that it's all for your good, and you'll find, in the end, that it was.

# BRAVE LOVE

*The Lord will not cast off forever.*
*Though He causes grief,*
*Yet He will show compassion*
*According to the multitude of His mercies.*
*For He does not afflict willingly,*
*Nor grieve the children of men.*
LAMENTATIONS 3:31–33 NKJV

Have you ever thought that God is much braver than we at allowing His children to face trouble? We try to keep our children from as many problems as possible. Some even overprotect thoroughly rebellious children by defending them from challenges that could cause growth.

In order to get the attention of a disobedient Christian, God does not hesitate to bring a measure of hurt into that life. For awhile He allows the defiant one to experience the well-earned fruits of disobedience. But He'll not allow grief to last forever. Eventually, as the perverse Christian turns and realizes the loss of God's intimate love, the Savior's multitude of mercies pour out again. Though He bravely allows His child to experience pain, it is only for a time.

Do you know someone who has walked away from God and struggles with the results of that choice? Recognize that God has not ended His love. Unlike many people, He has not written that soul off as impossible to reclaim. But also, do not take too lightly the fact that this suffering is caused by sin. Don't excuse it when you see it, or tell that believer that wrongdoing has nothing to do with life's troubles.

Yet God's blessings are available to even the most disobedient child who turns from sin. Pray for that loved one to turn again and accept the Savior's love. Over and over again God gave that blessing to Israel and Judah. He'll give it to those you love, too.

# FOLLOW THE LEADER

*"For I say to you, that unless your righteousness*
*exceeds the righteousness of the scribes and Pharisees,*
*you will by no means enter the kingdom of heaven."*
MATTHEW 5:20 NKJV

Jesus discouraged His followers from taking the rule-following scribes and Pharisees for their model. Though they might have impressed first-century Jews, these folks didn't even begin to stir God's Son, because He knew they only sought to make points with God, not develop a relationship with Him and serve Him with all their lives. The Jewish leaders were simply trying to play games with holiness.

Before we start picking on them, though, recognize that on our own, none of us can do better than the scribes and Pharisees. We, too, try to "do right" and end up getting caught in more rules. In a short time, we're bogged down in how to do things, not whom to love.

So Jesus went on to point out the wickedness that fills all our hearts unless His Spirit has control. Guidelines on how to be a Christian, rigorously adhered to, still won't change anger, lust, or hard-heartedness. As we read the verses that follow this, all of us become aware of our own weakness.

Had God left us to earn our own salvation, we'd be truly desperate. We couldn't be the light of the world that He calls us to be earlier in this chapter. But when we recognize that He controls all the world and that our hearts are part of it, when we submit ourselves to His will instead of finding our own solutions, His Spirit leads us in a love relationship that changes hearts and minds.

Then, we're not following any leader but Him, and that's just the way it should be.

# UNEARNED

*"You are the light of the world.*
*A city that is set on a hill cannot be hidden."*
MATTHEW 5:14 NKJV

I magine if God required us to earn our own salvation, as many religions or misunderstandings of Christianity imply. Earning our place in heaven would be a weighty thing. When we woke each morning, our minds would fill with ways we could assure our acceptance with God. We'd probably start with a laundry list of things to do in order to assure our places in heaven. Whenever we had free time, we'd be trying to slip in a few good deeds.

But when those well-meant good deeds went awry, would we chalk them up to a sin-filled world or berate ourselves for having done wrong when we planned on doing right? How would we escape from the world's tendency to make even good things fall apart?

The harder we tried, the more we'd focus on ourselves, our failings, and our need to do better. Instead of reaching out to others because God loved them, we'd try to touch them to improve our own heavenly lot. Selfishness would impede all we did.

That's why God doesn't expect us to earn our way into heaven. He settled that issue when He gave us the gift of salvation and freed us to become His light in the world, reflecting the light of His Son, who came to illuminate our lives with knowledge of Him.

Free of the need to secure a place in eternity, we devote ourselves to spreading His light, selflessly sharing the way to the Father whose gift means all to us. Set high above the earn-your-way-into-heaven crowd, we shine brightly and light the path to eternal security in Jesus.

# EITHER/OR

*The way of the LORD is strength for the upright,*
*But destruction will come to the workers of iniquity.*
PROVERBS 10:29 NKJV

Scripture, especially Proverbs, has a lot of these either/or statements, which basically say you can love God and have this blessing, or you can avoid, ignore, and even hate Him and receive this bad thing.

God offers plenty of blessings to those who love Him. He showers us with good things because He is a good God who wants to share much with us and give us joy. But those who refuse Him receive quite another response from God. They would misuse the strength (or other gifts) He offers. Instead of doing right in the world, they'd make a mess of it. So God withholds good from them and seeks to limit their ability to do harm.

Some may complain that God picks on unbelievers. *Why,* they may wonder, *should they receive destruction instead of at least moderately nice things?* Read Matthew 5:45, which points out that God allows some good things to happen to both the just and the unjust person. No one is completely cut off from pleasant things, but God will not give His enemies an unfair advantage or allow them complete control of His loved ones.

Have no doubt about it, this is a war, albeit a spiritual one. Though the last battle may be long off, God takes the conflict seriously. Destruction for those who hate Him is the ultimate end.

But strength, given to believers, allows them to fight on when the enemy seems strong. Blessings are the reinforcements that enable us to go on when the battle becomes hard.

God always gives the right things to the right people—those who trust in Him.

# GLORIOUS SONG

*Then Moses and the children of Israel sang
this song to the LORD, and spoke, saying:
"I will sing to the LORD, for He has triumphed gloriously!
The horse and its rider He has thrown into the sea!"*
EXODUS 15:1 NKJV

Has there been a day when you felt like throwing a praise party in your heart? Perhaps it came on the day Jesus entered your heart with a *whoosh* and cleaned out the debris of sin. Or maybe you celebrated a wonderful experience and simply had to give God the glory.

Then you can understand why the Israelites, who had just seen their enemies defeated by the Red Sea, simply had to stop and sing. Praise was the order of the day as they completely trusted in the One who liberated them from slavery.

Has God thrown something in the sea for you? If you're a Christian, that must be true, for your sins have been tossed into the deep where no one can retrieve them. Now you stand on the opposite shore, separated from that awful past in which Satan ruled your life.

So don't go fishing in the Red Sea, trying to retrieve those past wrongs. Don't attempt to return to Egypt when the Promised Land lies before you. Instead, stop on the shore, sing praise to God to show your thankfulness, then head out for the new land God offers.

You may have to cross some dry places before you enter it, but God will see you through. Just remember to stop and sing a few praises on the way, as He continues to help you on.

# SPIRIT FLOW

*Jesus said to her, "I am the resurrection and the life.*
*He who believes in Me, though he may die, he shall live."*
JOHN 11:25 NKJV

Coming to Jesus brings us new life. Not just a few more years on earth or a better way of living, but real, exciting, wonderful life. Existence free from the necessity of constant sin. The ability to do right things for the right reasons.

As the resurrection does its work in our lives, we receive life from death. God didn't send His Son to die for us so that we could improve our lives, make better choices, or feel good about ourselves. We, who had no life beyond a meager existence on earth with a few years of struggle and suffering, now have the kind of life God intended us to have all along—eternal, blessed life, life connected to Himself.

Without Jesus, though people live physically, they have no spiritual life. It's as if an empty shell is walking around, making mistakes and existing in confusion. But when God's Spirit fills that shell to the point of bursting, when His energy overflows from that once-empty spot, we know what it's like to really live.

No matter what we experience in life, as long as we're connected closely to Jesus, that vitality will burst out again. Sometimes, when we struggle, it may seem to barely fill us. But as God's resurrection power works again and again in our beings, the Spirit leaks, pushes, and flows out again.

Though we die, the Spirit will not leave us. Nothing separates us from God's eternal life.

# KEEPING THE WORD

*"Most assuredly, I say to you, if anyone keeps My word*
*he shall never see death."*
JOHN 8:51 NKJV

When Jesus spoke these words, the Jews thought He was mad. The very idea that He was greater than Abraham offended these outwardly faithful Jews. They didn't like the idea that Jesus claimed that much authority.

But these words are obviously a challenge to anyone. They fly in the face of the "practical" world we live in. We don't think Jesus lost His mind, but do we have a challenge believing that eternal life is really ours? Are we tempted to believe in things that aren't contained in His Word? Do we struggle to believe that the way He laid out for belief in God is really *the* way—the only way?

Jesus doesn't simply say that those who never see death believe in His Word. Many people can give some mental assent to His teachings, though their hearts haven't been converted. Others have walked the aisle but failed to follow through. Jesus doesn't want people who have followed the "right" formulas. He wants those whose hearts, minds, and spirits are engaged with Him and willing to act on His words.

Those who do that receive a great promise—eternal life, uncounted ages in which to draw even nearer to the One whose Word meant so much in the hours, days, and years of earthly life. Keeping His Word may cost something today, but this world's price will never compare with unending benefits in an eternity of salvation. So when we struggle to keep our faith on track, trust fully in all Jesus said, and live consistently with the Scriptures, let's remind ourselves where we're heading: Heaven is our real home.

# GENEROUS GIVER

*"Ask, and it will be given to you;*
*seek, and you will find;*
*knock, and it will be opened to you."*
MATTHEW 7:7 NKJV

Have you ever had anyone offer to give as generously to you as Jesus? If so, did that human follow through on every promise with all you wanted or needed? Not really. No one can give the way Jesus can. People don't have His assets, and even if they did, they can't reach all the hurting places of the heart or give perfect guidance. Jesus not only wants to give, He gives all we need.

Our huge, aching void, a collection of unmet needs present a problem to us, or any human. But to Jesus, they are an opportunity to fill us with His love. Or where we cannot forgive, He can empty those closets filled with fear and doubt and replace them with overflowing compassion.

But He doesn't promise to give all we want in a moment. The Christian walk is one of asking, seeking, and knocking. No spoiled children enter heaven, untried and replete with too many good things. God wants us to value the gifts He gives, and anything received too easily is also easily despised. Though He gives wholeheartedly and offers only the best, Jesus will have nothing unappreciated.

When we look back at our lives, will we view a life of thanks for gifts God sent quickly, barely in time, or incredibly slowly, in our opinion? Whether we merely asked, sought, or knocked incessantly, at the end of our lives we'll certainly realize that everything came just in time—God's time. And our praises will ring through all the earth.

# FILLED SPIRIT

*"Blessed are the poor in spirit,*
*For theirs is the kingdom of heaven."*
MATTHEW 5:3 NKJV

These words describe someone with a character just the opposite of the scribes and Pharisees—respected Jews who would soon become Jesus' main enemies. Though these leaders talked a lot about God, made every effort to look good, and probably had excellent reputations, Jesus described them as "whitewashed tombs" (Matthew 23:27). They might have looked good on the outside, but inside they were disgusting.

Maybe you've met some folks who thought they had a great spiritual life, were proud of their place in the community, and talked a good line about their faith, yet they never cracked open a Bible and lived according to their own rules, not God's. Full of their own spiritual importance, they may not have listened when you tried to tell them about real faith.

These so-called spiritually full people head toward destruction at Mach speed, though they don't recognize it. They can't hear Jesus calling them to recognize their own emptiness, instead, and fly to Him for filling.

Only those who know their own inadequacy, when it comes to pleasing God, are ready to be truly full. Instead of clinging to ideas that cannot save or trying to earn their way into heaven, they recognize that all they can offer cannot make them ready for eternity. God must drain them of their own "spiritual" ideas, values, and desires first.

Those who recognize that truth and turn to Jesus are filled with His Spirit and given a new life. Eventually they inherit heaven with Him. But from that first breath of new life, heaven lies within their hearts, and God's filling has begun.

# SHARE THE BLESSING

*"Blessed are those who mourn,*
*For they shall be comforted."*
MATTHEW 5:4 NKJV

Do you fear mourning? Naturally no one prefers to go through suffering, but it is nothing to be dreaded. Jesus maintains it is actually what we would call a blessing in disguise.

Those who have experienced mourning with Jesus by their sides can attest to the truth of His claim. Anyone who has never mourned and felt the constant, faithful support of this Best Friend cannot appreciate the good that comes from mourning—the proved trust that Jesus will always be faithful, the knowledge that nothing can separate the believer from the Savior. Those who have felt the arm of the Lord around them in sorrow have proved this promise again and again.

Has Jesus comforted you? Pass on what you received. While others doubt, question, and fall into gloom, if you've held the Savior's hand through a great loss, you can encourage mourners.

What have you lost: A loved one? A job you enjoyed? Some physical blessing provided by God? Has God stood by you, despite the suffering? Tactfully offer God's comfort to hurting people who face a similar faith challenge. Do not fear gently sharing His faithfulness and offering to pray for the pained soul. God sometimes acts alone, but He most often works through the mouths and hands of His people. Suffering ones yearn to hear that God has aided others and will also help them. You can tell them His promises are as true today as they were when He spoke them.

As you share the blessing, God will also bless you. It's always a joy to tell of the love of Jesus. Let your mouth and spirit be filled with the joy of God's fulfilled promise.

# BLESSED MERCY

*"Blessed are the merciful,*
*For they shall obtain mercy."*
MATTHEW 5:7 NKJV

Give mercy, and you will receive it—that's often true in our world, and it's even more true in eternal terms.

As Christians, we have received God's great mercy. We cannot complain no one offered us compassion, because He gave us so much in one large package marked "salvation." All our sins are behind His back, never to be brought to our attention again. Yet His mercy didn't end there. Daily He renews His gifts as we live for Him. As we wake each morning and go to sleep every night, we can thank Him for His watchful care and ask His forgiveness all over again for the wrongs of the day.

Should we hold on to our mercy and not pass it on to any we come in contact with each day, we betray God's work. He didn't offer us forgiveness for our sins so that we could hold a grudge against another or demand the final payment for every sin against us. Acting that way ruins our Christian testimony. Satan's the one who demands full payment for every wrong, not God. The Savior offers the blessing of forgiveness, based on His life's sacrifice.

But when we offer mercy to others, not only does God approve, people often recognize the good we've done and are more likely to give us a break, too. The forgiven offender is likely to be less critical of us when we make mistakes. The one we've helped is usually willing to help us out when we're in a pinch.

This ebb and flow of mercy is just what God had in mind. Mercy, passed around the world by kindhearted Christians, changes a lot of attitudes and hearts.

# SIN STRUGGLE

*And now, all glory to God, who is able to keep you from stumbling,*
*and who will bring you into his glorious presence innocent of sin*
*and with great joy. All glory to him, who alone is God our Savior,*
*through Jesus Christ our Lord. Yes, glory, majesty, power, and authority*
*belong to him, in the beginning, now, and forevermore. Amen.*

JUDE 24–25 NLT

As Christians, we often easily recognize our own lack of perfection. Sin still mars our lives, though we make many efforts to keep it at bay. But think of it from another angle. If we didn't know God, we'd commit even more sin. Jude reminds us that God keeps us from stumbling.

Struggling with a besetting sin? Don't give up. God hasn't. The glorious Savior is working to bring you into His way. Today you may stumble less than before, and years from now, this temptation may lose its hold on you.

That doesn't give us an excuse to ignore His commands or knowingly do wrong. Instead, it's an opportunity to recognize that we never walk alone when temptation threatens. Jesus is nearby, waiting to help, if only we call out to Him.

As sin begins to lose its grip, our lives increasingly reflect His glory. We stumble less and reap the benefits of righteous living as our lives both please God and ourselves. The pain of sin has less and less impact on us, and our hearts are filled with joy.

This new way of living is not simply a result of our own efforts. Apart from Jesus, the glorious One with authority over the world— and our lives—it could never have happened.

Let's glorify His majesty and power again.

# LOOKING AHEAD

*For our present troubles are quite small and won't last very long.*
*Yet they produce for us an immeasurably great glory*
*that will last forever!*

2 CORINTHIANS 4:17 NLT

Have you ever watched a reality TV show where contestants went through all kinds of awful stunts in order to win large amounts of money? Why would anyone do such a thing? Because the promise of the money lured them so strongly that they were willing to do almost anything to get it.

Greed may be a powerful motivator, but it isn't a perfect one. As those shows prove, eventually, most people draw a line at something. It's not worth it to put life and health at risk for a huge chunk of change. But you can get most people to do a certain number of distasteful things for a big benefit.

Christians know what it means to suffer for awhile to get something even better. But we have a finer motivation than money. Today we go through some troubles—we decide not to take a job that wouldn't please Jesus or we receive mocking from others because we tell of our faith. Some believers even die for their faithful testimony. Why do we put up with such things? Because we look forward to something much better than a big check—our eyes focus on eternity with Jesus.

Yet even those who give up their earthly lives discover that compared to eternity it was only a small trouble. What could compare to spending "immeasurably great glory" with the Savior?

# NEED STRENGTH?

*Seek the LORD and His strength; Seek His face evermore!*
1 CHRONICLES 16:11 NKJV

Need strength? You know where to go: Look to Jesus.

Are you confused, hurting, doubtful? Any emotion you feel, He can relate to. During His years on earth, He learned about them all. Nothing comes as a surprise to Him.

Do you feel as if you can't go on? He can keep you going by His power, and as His Spirit fills you, you'll know that even if you're fighting tooth and nail, you'll eventually win in Him.

Whatever we face, God wants to share His strength with us. His might is not simply something He plans on using to make us see things His way or manipulate us into a position where He'll be in control. It's a powerful blessing He has designed to share with us.

As we get to know Jesus more closely—as we peer into His face and understand more completely just who He is—we are awed by His strength and humbled by His desire to share even that with us. But as we recognize those truths, we also understand that all the strength we have is loaned to us by Him. Misusing it is never an option as we draw near and thank Him for the way He allows His power to work in our lives.

Have you felt the power of Jesus in your life? If not, draw closer to Him. The more you seek Him, the more His strength can empower all your life.

# STANDING IN STRENGTH

*Strength and honor are her clothing;*
*She shall rejoice in time to come.*
PROVERBS 31:25 NKJV

In a day when dishonesty is often almost taken as a matter of course, a woman whose strength of character demands honesty can stand out in a crowd. Sometimes it's the kind of standing out she'd prefer not to have when her strength leads to uncomfortable situations. A worker who refuses to lie for her boss or to a client or a politician who stands firm on her promises may get some grief and even experience some losses. But no matter how hard it seems, clothing herself in strength and honesty is still the right thing to do. If she stands firm, Scripture promises, she'll be glad of it in the end.

Doing right doesn't always make life easy. Many who go with the flow don't appreciate being confronted with their own expendable morals. When an honorable person stands firm against them, they'll attack with all they have and may even try to dislodge the honest one. Right actions can cause Christians to feel intense heat from others.

But that doesn't mean their stance is wrong. There are things worth standing firm for, even if they have a price. Sometimes that price, painful as it may seem, is just what brings the blessing.

Because no matter how intensely people may attack the strong and honorable woman, He who holds on to her future never will. God may not remove the trouble immediately, but He will eventually bring the blessing, and when that happens, her trials will be entirely worth it.

Are you clothed in strength and honor? Have you begun to pay the price of that faithfulness? Stand firm. In awhile, you'll be rejoicing.

# RIGHTEOUS LORD

*The Lord is righteous in her midst,*
*He will do no unrighteousness.*
*Every morning He brings His justice to light;*
*He never fails, but the unjust knows no shame.*
ZEPHANIAH 3:5 NKJV

The completely rebellious, shameless people of Jerusalem hadn't listened to God, trusted in Him, or wanted to spend any time with Him. As God's chosen people, they were pretty much failures, because they'd chosen anything rather than Him.

Had God reacted to them like a human, in unrighteous anger, this city, which should have been the star of His nation, probably would have been history. Humanly speaking, they didn't deserve His compassion. But God responds to us not on the basis of our sin, but on His nature. Though His people became unrighteous, the Lord could not be anything but just and compassionate.

But sometimes love allows the rebellious ones to have their way for a time. For many years, God allowed that nation to follow its own will. But one day, He promised, Judah would see the justice God committed to. Then, He told them, they would walk with Him, and all His judgments for their disobedience would end. They would be glad again, in deep relationship with Him.

When we read this passage, we, too, can be glad. We've had our own rebellious moments. Like the people of Jerusalem, judgment could have been our end. But in God's mercy, He gave us His Son, who walks with us and shows us the light of His love. Though we slip away from Him, He calls us home again. Every morning, we can return to Him.

# FAITHFUL ONES

*"The LORD your God in your midst,*
*The Mighty One, will save;*
*He will rejoice over you with gladness,*
*He will quiet you with His love,*
*He will rejoice over you with singing."*
ZEPHANIAH 3:17 NKJV

Have you ever thought of the joy Jesus has in you? It's been of real benefit for you to know Him—of course His salvation makes you glad—but have you ever wondered why God would be glad to have a foible-filled human life in His hands? Because when we come to Jesus, our lives have been terribly marred by sin.

Trying to figure out why God delights so much in us could strain our minds with mental pain. Small as we are, we cannot understand His thoughts or motivations. But one thing we know for certain, the unendingly creative Lord we serve does not leave our lives messed up. Instead He saves us and creates a new life, where once there was wickedness and confusion. Before we've even begun to obey, He's glad to do it, and His love and rejoicing don't die as we grow in Him—Jesus always rejoices in His people and brings them peace in many ways. Just as the Lord rejoiced in those of Judah who trusted in Him, He revels in today's believers. God doesn't save anyone whom He will not consistently delight in.

So on those days when you're faithful but unfulfilled, feeling miserable and unloved, when no one shares your joys or encourages you in hardship, don't despair. Jesus is rejoicing with you, comforting you, and singing joyfully at your faithful service to Him.

Jesus always rejoices in His faithful ones.

# THIRSTY?

*Some wandered in the desert, lost and homeless.*
*Hungry and thirsty, they nearly died.*
*"LORD, help!" they cried in their trouble,*
*and he rescued them from their distress.*
PSALM 107:4–6 NLT

Even those who may not be homeless or running about a desert looking for shelter relate to this verse. People can find themselves "homeless" in many ways. In fact, we all more or less are that way from the day we're born. God created us to be at home in Him, and until we come to Him in faith, we wander in a desert of false religion and self-sufficiency.

Whether or not you have a handsome home to go to, life can get pretty dry and purposeless if you don't know Jesus. You can see it in the people caught up in addictions because their lives have gone wrong and they don't know how to set them right. You see it in the outwardly perfect family suddenly torn apart by one member's sin.

God wants to rescue even the most lost and homeless, the ones whose tongues are stuck to the roofs of their mouths with thirst or who are about to perish from lack of liquid. No one is too dry for God to revive. All it requires from the thirsty one is the realization that thirst for Him is the problem, and a cry of "help" the solution. God sends in His rescuing Spirit, and new, refreshed life begins.

Are you parched for God's Spirit? Call on Him now. Even those who already know Him can feel dry and empty. All who sincerely call on Him will feel His powerful touch.

# RIVER OF LOVE

*He changes rivers into deserts, and springs of water into dry land.*
*But he also turns deserts into pools of water,*
*the dry land into flowing springs.*
PSALM 107:33, 35 NLT

Dry to wet or wet to dry, God changes the world at His will, ruling over it in ways we often don't understand. Though scientists spend time in labs or the environment seeking to understand creation, we lag distantly behind the Lord who commands it. Much in His incredibly complex world eludes our understanding.

But deserts and rivers aren't the only things God rules. Though we may question or rebel against this truth, God also rules our lives. Even the most wicked of us cannot go farther than God allows, and even the best of us only has so many years to do good works.

What's true of creation is true of us: We, too, are incredibly complex. Our hearts may hurt for years over a series of wrongs; as they work deep into our souls, they work on our spirits and thoughts in convoluted ways. We may not even understand why we hurt, yet we see the results in our lives.

But just as God perfectly understands our world, He sees into our hurt hearts and spirits. And He can alter a river of hate or doubt into springs of faith and trust. Though that heart change may not happen overnight, with faith and determination to follow God's Word, we can see amazing changes.

As God's healing water seeps into our lives, the trickle touches our souls and change becomes possible. But as we open ourselves to His will and way, the trickle springs up, becomes a stream, a pool, then a river of love.

And all of it started in God's hand.

# PLANNING MODE

*You chart the path ahead of me and tell me where to stop and rest.*
*Every moment you know where I am.*

PSALM 139:3 NLT

Are you the kind of person who likes to plan out your life to the last minute? Or are you so go-with-the-flow that you rarely look ahead more than a short time? No matter what your style, you need one path charted through life. When you walk with God, whether you're a down-to-the-minute planner or a let's-see sort, a plan is always at work in your life. He goes before you to plot the most successful course, show you the way, and make sure you reach your destination.

Most human plans plot a fast and furious course to get to the goal in the shortest amount of time. But God's itinerary is different. He creates rest stops for the weary soul. No person can go on forever without a break. No one can go that directly to a serious objective and not pay the price.

When we make our plans, we need to take God's goals into account. A strategy that follows His laws and includes spiritual aims heads us in the right direction, but one that takes no account for His designs lands us on a path leading to destruction—or at least disappointment.

Have you wondered why a plan didn't work as you expected? Did you make it with God's will, as well as your own, in mind? Are you trusting Him to lead you in the right way? Or are you fighting Him when He has ordained a period of rest? Remind yourself that yours is not the final plan—His is. Since He knows the final goal, He'll always send you in the right direction.

# ALWAYS BLESSED

*In the day of prosperity be joyful,*
*But in the day of adversity consider:*
*Surely God has appointed the one as well as the other,*
*So that man can find out nothing that will come after him.*
ECCLESIASTES 7:14 NKJV

Sometimes our souls don't feel particularly satisfied. If we lose a job, wonder how we'll pay the rent, and imagine all kinds of dire results, it's hard to feel very peaceful. Prosperous days seem to lie behind us, and we can't look into the future and tell how long we'll be in this situation.

God doesn't allow us to look into the future. That's a good thing, because if we knew the future, we wouldn't need to trust God. One of His best methods of developing our spiritual lives would no longer exist, and we'd enter heaven as weak, spineless beings, not the strong ones He wants to create.

But just as God ordained good things in our prosperous times, He brings good even from our most challenging moments. Unemployment may provide a time for spiritual deepening in many ways, as we cling more firmly to Him and know that all we receive comes directly from His hand. When our days are not filled with work at an office or shop, some temporary ministry may appear.

But whether we are joyful or sad, God still remains faithful. He provides our needs, even if we don't get the lavish things we'd prefer. And He always provides generous spiritual blessings for those who trust in Him. Like Paul, who experienced prosperity and want, we can do all things, when we abound in Him (Philippians 4:12–13).

No matter what your circumstances, you can always cling to Jesus—and be blessed.

# CHURCH SERVICE

*Looking unto Jesus the author and finisher of our faith;*
*who for the joy that was set before him endured the cross,*
*despising the shame, and is set down at the right hand*
*of the throne of God.*
HEBREWS 12:2 KJV

What makes a church really successful? I'm not talking about numbers, converts, or depth of programs for different ages, but the kind of church that really gets at the heart of faith.

Different people might answer that question various ways. And many of their responses might have validity. But I submit that the one that is successful in Jesus' eyes is the church that looks intently to Him, recognizing the importance of His sacrifice in their own lives and the need of all to come to Him.

Many congregations claim to be Christian, but how many are seeking Jesus' face? How many understand the critical importance of Jesus and His sacrifice so that we may have eternal life? Some Christians will be stunned that the questions even needs to be asked. They've grown up in strong churches and heard the gospel all their lives. But many who spend lots of years in "church" have never heard the gospel or gotten its message that only through Jesus can anyone come to God.

A church isn't successful because it sends out missionaries, addresses social issues, or claims to believe in the Scriptures. Those are all part of the testimony of the church, but none is the main focus. The only real focus of faith is Jesus, and when we glorify Him, draw close to Him, and recognize our emptiness without Him, we are the real church—the one He rejoiced to serve with His life.

Who—or what—are you serving today?

# ALL GOD'S CHILDREN

*If God doesn't discipline you as he does all of his children,*
*it means that you are illegitimate and*
*are not really his children after all.*

Hebrews 12:8 NLT

How does God's discipline feel? Knowing that God doesn't approve of what we're doing may be painful. Most of us would rather have Jesus' commendation than chastisement. But all of us have times when He brings to our attention something we've done wrong or an important truth we've missed.

Though we may not think it, that's a time to rejoice in the fact that God loves us. He shows that love by telling us we need to make helpful changes. If He were a less caring Father, He'd let us go on our own way, make many disastrous mistakes, and learn everything the hard way. But He's not cruel, so He lets us in on the things that could hurt us if we kept on doing them. He corrects *all* His children.

Criticism from a well-meaning friend may hurt, and we may not know whether to believe all that loved one says. But redirection from God is never done with a mean spirit and never contains biases or untruths. Whatever He tells us to do, we can trust in completely.

If someone tells you God has never provided such direction in his or her life, wonder if that person has really made a commitment to Jesus. Because this verse tells us that only those who don't truly know Him are never disciplined. God only corrects those He loves, so rejoice when He sets you on the right path—He loves you, and He's showing you the best way to live.

# PERSONAL REJECTION

*As a tongue of fire consumes stubble*
*And dry grass collapses into the flame,*
*So their root will become like rot and their blossom blow away as dust;*
*For they have rejected the law of the LORD of hosts*
*And despised the word of the Holy One of Israel.*
ISAIAH 5:24 NASB

When I was a young Christian, a mentor told me God takes it very personally when we reject His Word. That's been an important personal truth, but it's also one that benefits all Christians in many ways.

We may not automatically put a lot of stock in the Bible, but God takes His Word very seriously, even to the point of punishing His own people when they ignore His truths. Scripture reveals so much about Him—it tells us much about His character, describing who He is and how He acts, and gives to us an understanding of the best way we can live if we want a close relationship with Him.

When we ignore or denigrate His Word, we're telling God we don't want a relationship with Him or we want to remain as distant as possible from Him while claiming His name. Of course He won't take that affront calmly. If no human wants to be ignored or abused that way, imagine how the Lord of glory feels when those whom He created act as if He's unimportant.

No wonder God punishes those who treat Him so cavalierly. " 'Do not My words do good to him who walks uprightly?' " God asked the prophet Micah (2:7 NKJV). All God planned was to do good for people, and they rejected Him.

Why receive punishment when good is offered to those who take His Word seriously? Commit instead to faith that receives the best Jesus has to offer.

# PURE HEARTED

*Truly God is good to Israel,*
*To such as are pure in heart.*
PSALM 73:1 NKJV

"God is good." Recently I had a day when God seemed to repeat this truth over and over in the mouths of others and my own mind. It was surely a day of blessing when I appreciated all He'd done for me. I felt as if praise bubbled over on that day, barely contained in all I did.

You don't hear that sentiment from the hearts of unbelievers, who are more likely to ask where God is when trouble strikes or wonder why some unpleasant things happen. Only believers who have appreciated His work in their lives are likely to sing His praises this way.

That's just who the pure in heart are—those whom His Spirit has cleansed and in whose lives He is working every day. Though God provides some things to those who deny Him—a beautiful world, rain in season, and food to keep them alive—they take it for granted and as their due. Thanks rarely pass their lips, though complaints may often be found there.

When we feel God's goodness in our lives, are we quick to share it with others? Do we rejoice when God keeps a friend from harm or meets a special need? Then our pure hearts are shared with the world. Let's not hold back a word of praise from a filthy-hearted world that desperately needs cleansing. Our gentle testimony may be just the thing that turns a heart to God.

When we hear of that cleansing, again we'll be saying, "Truly, God is good."

# RIVER OF FAITH

*Jesus stood and cried out, saying,*
*"If anyone thirsts, let him come to Me and drink.*
*He who believes in Me, as the Scripture has said,*
*out of his heart will flow rivers of living water."*
JOHN 7:37–38 NKJV

Are you thirsty? Drink deeply of Jesus. He's the only water you can imbibe that will never require additional drafts. Consume $H_2O$ and a few hours later, at the most, you'll be returning to a faucet or bottle for more. Quaff deeply of Jesus, and a river of His love will always be available to you.

Those listening to Jesus knew real thirst. They lived in a dry, desert climate. No one had running water, so every day the women of the household carried large jars to the well, dipped into its depths, pulled the water up, and carried home those heavy containers. Even getting water could be hot and thirsty work.

We may not carry water, but we've felt the desperate spiritual thirst Jesus describes here. Sin weighs us down, drains hope from our hearts, and leaves us empty. We search for a solution and find it in Him.

Once we've tasted Jesus, we need no other well to drink from— no spiritual guru who claims to have hidden answers, no seer or psychic to show us the future. The "water" they offer would leave us thirsting again in no time, and we'd have nothing to offer others.

All our hopes lie in the One who provides rivers of truth to water our hungry souls. When we've drunk deeply, His river overflows our lives and splashes into the hearts and minds of those we live and work with. Their thirst quenched, they convey it on to others, and the river of faith swells again.

# MIND-HEART COVENANT

*"This is the covenant that I will make with the house of Israel after those days, says the LORD: I will put My law in their minds, and write it on their hearts; and I will be their God, and they shall be My people."*

JEREMIAH 31:33 NKJV

It's hard for us to imagine what living under the Old Testament law was like. We read the multitude of laws God gave His people, and our minds boggle at how anyone could follow every one.

When we feel that way, we're in just the place God had in mind for His people. God knew that following all those laws would make all humanity aware of the distance between their own feeble abilities and God's greatness. The rules and regulations would keep them mindful of how impossible pleasing God by doing good was. Animal sacrifices would help them understand the awfulness of sin.

But God also knew that all the Old Testament truths would still leave a gap between Him and His people, so He promised that one day, instead of simply reading the law, they would have it in their minds and hearts. It would become vibrant in their lives.

As Christians, we don't simply follow rules, waiting for a day when faith will be written on our hearts. God's given that promise, with the coming of the Spirit in our lives. Jesus commands our hearts and minds. We aren't simply rule driven, though we constantly seek to obey our Lord's commands. Because we love Jesus, we obey His Word.

God gave His law to bless us, not to confuse our minds. He wants to fill our hearts with joy. Then we know the real blessing of a mind-heart covenant with Him.

# LIGHTEN YOUR DAY

*Let Israel rejoice in their Maker;*
*Let the children of Zion be joyful in their King.*
PSALM 149:2 NKJV

On a slow, lethargic day, when a cold is taking over your being, or a day when things seem slightly out of control, a reminder that even in this Jesus is King can turn your day around in a remarkable way.

As your spirit lifts with that truth, your burdens may not be removed from your shoulders, your body may not experience immediate healing, yet your heart lightens with hope.

What changed? Nothing but the focus of your heart, which suddenly rejoices at who the Savior is. At the start of your pain, He was King, and He will be when it passes. But now, even as your nose drips or your throat hurts, or the problem annoys you, you feel more than personal sorrow. Attending to a larger reality than your own, praise raises your heart to a heavenly place that lasts longer than any momentary worldly irritation.

Jesus makes less-than-glorious days wonderful when we rejoice in Him. This psalm doesn't require a bright, sunny day, filled with good news. It calls us to praise without reference to our own condition.

You see, praise doesn't depend on us. Our daily trials aren't the focus of it, and our situations won't change the need for it. The Maker, who rules universes with the flick of a finger, is greater than a cold, a bad day at work, or a fleeting family problem. He holds solutions for them all in His hand.

Even on a gloomy, down day, we can rejoice in King Jesus, who easily bears even these light burdens. As we recognize this, that "bad" day shines in His glorious light.

# PROMISE KEEPER

*"But go, tell His disciples—and Peter—that He is going before you
into Galilee; there you will see Him, as He said to you."*

MARK 16:7 NKJV

The women went to the tomb, ready to prepare Jesus' body with spices, but instead met an angel, who reminded them of Jesus' promise. Perhaps they shouldn't have been so surprised; after all, Jesus had warned them. But who among us can honestly say we would hear such a message and respond more faithfully? If we'd seen the events the disciples faced, would we have jumped to this conclusion?

God always has the ability to surprise us. We cannot put Him in a small box and expect Him to live there. We can never control Him or comfortably predict His actions. Like the disciples, we'll find that even when He's prepared the way by giving us warning or directions, His goodness and power can still overwhelm us. Either we don't understand or don't quite believe enough. Yet He completes His plan and pours out those seemingly impossible blessings. Nothing is impossible with God.

Do we live as if God really means what He says? When we read Scripture, do we believe He will provide all He promises? Can we trust that as His Spirit calls our hearts to action, He will empower us to complete the task?

Jesus kept all His first-century promises, and He hasn't changed in twenty centuries. He'll keep His word to us, too.

# WHY?

*What is man, that thou art mindful of him?*
*and the son of man, that thou visitest him?*
PSALM 8:4 KJV

This is one of those keep-you-up-at-night or make-you-zany questions that loom large in Scripture. If we're honest, and we look at our omnipotent, perfect Lord, we wonder why He should be mindful of us. It's not as if He somehow needs us the way we require Him. God could do fine, thank you, without our small, confused lives as interferences.

Why God chose to love such unlovely beings is one of Scripture's most awesome mysteries. Something inside the Merciful One compelled Him to a series of acts we humans would instantly recoil from. Suffering was not too high a price for Jesus, when the alternative was to leave us languishing in outer darkness for eternity. To draw people to Himself, Jesus willingly paid a huge personal price.

As confused as the psalmist may have felt about God's decision to take on such a costly and seemingly personally unbeneficial love, human ability to apprehend this truth has never increased. We continue the quest to understand God's grace. Thousands of years haven't answered the question, and it could be pondered by humanity for thousands more, without turning up a satisfying clue. The revelation exists in God Himself, His own immense, gracious Person, whom we struggle to understand.

On earth, we may never comprehend God's desire or plan, but through the ages, all Christians have joined in worship and praise of One who gives so willingly and generously. While we may never nail down God's motives, we can certainly rejoice in their results, as we experience overwhelming evidence of the Savior's love. Even without an answer, we love Him in return.

# COMING HOME

*I seek you with all my heart;*
*do not let me stray from your commands.*
PSALM 119:10

Like all my cats, Tuck came to me as a displaced stray. I've always wondered where he lived originally and what his life was like before he appeared in our driveway, starving and hurt. He might have lost a home because when he's not happy, he tends to knock things on the floor. I've lost some treasured items to his paw, when he wanted to be fed immediately and wasn't or wanted to leave a room that had the door closed. Obedience isn't this cat's strong point.

Humans aren't all that different from cats, really. We, too, tend to want what we want, when we want it. And when we don't get what we want, we may not smash every breakable item on a dresser, but we might shatter a few things in our lives.

When we act that way, God recognizes that it comes out of our own hurt and fear. But unlike a frustrated cat owner, He doesn't simply work around our emotions and put us in a safe place where we won't misbehave. Our heavenly Father takes us in and shows us that our own rule cages us in to misery. Then He offers us a better way—the path of love for Him, which gives us the freedom we've always sought.

As love for Jesus grows in our hearts, we seek to obey His every word, and love for Him constrains us from smashing our lives. With the psalmist, we ask to follow Him more completely.

God loves to hear His children pray that way. Heart-to-heart obedience to Jesus prepares our straying souls for their final, best home.

# THE FACE OF JESUS

*The LORD is my light and my salvation; whom shall I fear?*
*The LORD is the strength of my life; of whom shall I be afraid?*
PSALM 27:1 NKJV

Fear can so easily tie us up: fear of the future, when our lives seem out of control; dread that another will harm us or our loved ones; apprehension that we will make mistakes. The list could go on indefinitely and intimately. None of us is entirely fearless.

How powerfully fear attacks our lives, keeping us from doing the good acts we should, dragging us off into alleys of indecision, or leading us into wrongdoing. Yet our awesome God has told us not to fear. When we doubt and worry, He promises to be our strength. With Him beside us, we need have no concern that anyone could do us permanent harm.

Looking into His face, awed by the power behind this promise, we know that the idea of fear is ridiculous. But when we look away, do we remember His faithfulness to us? Or do issues in this world become so important we fall prey to their delusions? If that happens, we're looking in the wrong direction, putting our doubts before faith. We're letting people take the place of Jesus in our lives.

One look into His face, one touch of His power, and we know we've been wrong. So when earth tempts us, let us seek His face again. When He is our strength, we have nothing to fear at all. So why let that person stop us from doing what we know is right, from serving Jesus to the best of our abilities, or from taking a bold new step forward?

After all, whom should we fear, if He is our strength?

# GOODNESS AND MERCY

*Surely goodness and mercy shall follow me all the days of my life:*
*and I will dwell in the house of the LORD for ever.*

PSALM 23:6 KJV

God's goodness and mercy come in many packages and many sizes, but they follow us each day of our existence. Whether we've passed through many hard times or just a few, no day given to any believer following Jesus lacks these two blessings.

If you have faced many trials on earth, one day, when you reach heaven, you'll understand that God saved the best for last—in eternity, you'll discover He was simply giving you more honor and blessing in heaven. Nor if yours was a smoother life, will you be disappointed with your heavenly reward, if you remained faithful to the Savior, using your life to help those in need. God gives us different lives and blessings, designed just for us.

Those blessings provide goodness and mercy on earth and continued joy in heaven. There's no dissonance between our song here on earth and the one that will praise Jesus eternally. Anyone who serves Jesus with energy and love will come to eternity satisfied with His faithfulness. As we forever dwell in the house of the Lord whom we have served, we'll continue to experience His goodness in the real life of heaven—life that is not bombarded by sin or death.

If you love Jesus, goodness and mercy are on your trail today. Just make sure you're on the right track—the one He walked down before you.

# Inspirational Library

Beautiful purse/pocket-size editions of Christian classics bound in flexible leatherette. These books make thoughtful gifts for everyone on your list, including yourself!

*When I'm on My Knees*  The highly popular collection of devotional thoughts on prayer, especially for women.
Flexible Leatherette  $4.97

*The Bible Promise Book*  Over 1,000 promises from God's Word arranged by topic. What does God promise about matters like: Anger, Illness, Jealousy, Love, Money, Old Age, and Mercy? Find out in this book!
Flexible Leatherette  $3.97

*Daily Wisdom for Women*  A daily devotional for women seeking biblical wisdom to apply to their lives. Scripture taken from the New American Standard Version of the Bible.
Flexible Leatherette  $4.97

*My Daily Prayer Journal*  Each page is dated and features a Scripture verse and ample room for you to record your thoughts, prayers, and praises. One page for each day of the year.
Flexible Leatherette  $4.97

---

## Available wherever books are sold.

Or order from:
Barbour Publishing, Inc.
P.O. Box 719
Uhrichsville, OH 44683
www.barbourbooks.com

If you order by mail, add $2.00 to your order for shipping.
Prices are subject to change without notice.